AI IN RETAIL INDUSTRY

**Revolutionizing Customer Experience
and Supply Chains
 by Sayeed Siddiqui**

Copyright

Dedication

To all the retailers, builders, coders,
dreamers, and everyday problem solvers
transforming shop floors and cloud systems
alike—may AI be your most trusted ally.

And to Arpita Arya

Table of Contents

AI IN RETAIL INDUSTRY

Chapter 1

The Retail Renaissance: Enter AI

Retail is one of the oldest industries in human history, rooted in exchange, relationships, and the flow of goods and services to meet human needs. And yet today, it stands on the cusp of the greatest transformation it has ever seen. The driving force behind this change is not just the internet, mobile, or digital commerce—but something far more intelligent: artificial intelligence (AI).

AI is changing retail not just in terms of automation or efficiency—it is fundamentally reshaping *how*, *why*, and *what* consumers buy. From personalized recommendations and predictive inventory to voice-activated shopping and emotion-aware customer support, AI is powering a renaissance—reviving the retail experience, rebuilding it intelligently, and creating entirely new models of engagement.

1.1 – The Historical Shift

Retail has evolved through waves:

- **Artisan exchange** in early human settlements

- **Marketplace economies** in ancient Mesopotamia, Rome, and India

- **Guild-based trades** in medieval Europe

- **Department stores and catalogs** in the 19th century

- **Mass retail and supermarkets** in the 20th century

- **E-commerce** in the late 1990s

- **Mobile-first, omnichannel shopping** in the 2010s

- **AI-powered commerce** in the 2020s

Each shift was driven by technology, but the AI transformation is different. Unlike past tools that extended reach or added convenience, AI adds *cognition*—the ability for systems to learn, predict, and adapt.

This isn't just digitization. It's **intelligent transformation**.

1.2 – Why AI, Why Now?

Several forces are converging to make AI essential for retail:

- **Explosion of data**: Clicks, views, geolocation, sensor input, and transaction logs generate terabytes of retail data daily.

- **Cloud infrastructure**: Powerful computation now accessible on demand.

- **Open-source AI libraries**: Frameworks like TensorFlow, PyTorch, and Hugging Face have democratized development.

- **Customer expectations**: Shoppers now demand relevance, speed, and personalization as a baseline.

- **Pandemic acceleration**: COVID-19 forced digital transformation across every facet of retail operations.

The timing is critical. Retailers that delay AI adoption risk falling behind permanently—not just in innovation, but in profitability and customer trust.

1.3 – The Pillars of AI in Retail

AI creates value across all major retail functions:

1. **Customer Experience & Engagement**

   - Chatbots, voice assistants, personalized messaging

   - Sentiment-aware product recommendations

   - 24/7 smart customer service

2. **Merchandising & Inventory**

   - Demand forecasting and predictive replenishment

   - Smart product placement and pricing

   - AI-driven planograms and space utilization

3. **Supply Chain & Fulfillment**

- Route optimization

- Predictive logistics

- Real-time stock tracking and autonomous delivery

4. **Sales & Marketing**

   - Dynamic offers

   - Customer journey orchestration

   - A/B testing automation and ROI attribution

5. **Fraud Detection & Risk Management**

   - Anomaly detection in transactions

   - Predictive credit scoring

   - Bot protection and authentication via AI

1.4 – Real-World Use Cases

Let's look at how leading retailers are already deploying AI:

Amazon uses AI for product recommendations, fulfillment automation, voice commerce via Alexa, and predictive delivery—sometimes shipping before you click "buy."

- **Sephora** deploys AI and AR to let users try on makeup virtually, while AI scores help suggest ideal products by skin type and tone.

- **Zara** uses AI to analyze social media and store trends to design collections and predict regional demand.

- **Walmart** has AI bots scanning store shelves for restocking needs, and machine learning models helping schedule staff during peak hours.

- **Nike** employs AI to personalize shopping journeys, match shoes by foot scan, and build dynamic digital experiences in-store.

1.5 – Small Players, Big Tools

You don't need Amazon's budget to use AI.

AI is now accessible to **startups and SMBs** through:

- Shopify plugins with built-in AI

- Email marketing platforms using machine learning (like Klaviyo or Mailchimp)

- SaaS tools for image tagging, product discovery, and sentiment analysis

- No-code AI services like Microsoft Power Platform or Google AutoML

Even a boutique with a few SKUs can use AI to better forecast demand or suggest bundles that convert better.

1.6 – Mindset Shift: From Reactive to Predictive

Traditionally, retail was **reactive**:

- Stock what sold well last year

- Respond to customer complaints

- Set prices seasonally

AI flips that script. It enables **predictive, proactive, and personalized** action:

- Know what will sell next week

- Preempt returns by recommending the right fit

- Adjust prices in real time based on demand elasticity

This mindset isn't just operational—it's cultural. Retailers must think **in data loops**, not just sales cycles.

1.7 – AI Levels of Retail Maturity

AI maturity evolves through four stages:

1. **Awareness**: Experimenting with AI tools (e.g., using chatbots, analytics)

2. **Adoption**: Integrating AI into specific functions like marketing or inventory

3. **Alignment**: Connecting AI to broader business strategy

4. **AI-Native**: Designing the entire retail model around AI insights

Most companies are between stages 1 and 2. Leaders like Amazon, Alibaba, and Target are in stages 3 and 4.

1.8 – Barriers to Adoption

- **Data silos**: Fragmented customer, sales, and product data reduce AI accuracy

- **Legacy systems**: Old POS or ERP systems don't play well with new AI APIs

- **Lack of talent**: Few retail teams have dedicated AI specialists

- **Cost concerns**: AI is perceived as expensive, despite scalable options

- **Fear of job displacement**: AI is wrongly assumed to eliminate rather than augment roles

Overcoming these barriers requires leadership vision, strong cross-functional collaboration, and a commitment to upskilling staff.

1.9 – The AI Retail Ecosystem

AI thrives when connected to a strong stack:

- **Customer Data Platform (CDP)**

- **Enterprise Resource Planning (ERP)**

- **POS and eCommerce platforms**

- **Supply Chain Management (SCM)**

- **Marketing Automation and CRM**

- **Business Intelligence Tools**

AI doesn't work in isolation—it **amplifies** whatever ecosystem it joins.

1.10 – The Road Ahead: What This Book Will Cover

In the coming chapters, we'll cover:

- The foundational AI tools for retail success

- How customer experience is evolving with AI

- Personalization, pricing, and inventory optimization

- New job roles and workforce transformation

- Emerging technologies like AR/VR and robotics

- Ethical risks, privacy, and explainability

- Startup innovation and enterprise case studies

- A roadmap to launch or grow your AI retail career or business

1.11 – Conclusion: Welcome to Intelligent Commerce

AI is no longer a futuristic concept—it's the foundation of modern retail.

The leaders of tomorrow won't just use AI—they'll build with it, around it, and through it. Whether you're a retail employee, entrepreneur, executive, or analyst, this book will help you navigate the retail renaissance already underway.

Welcome to a world where every store is smarter, every touchpoint is personal, and every decision is driven by insight.

Welcome to *AI in Retail*.

Chapter 2

Understanding the AI Toolbox

Before retailers can deploy AI to revolutionize customer experience, pricing, supply chain, or personalization, they must understand the core tools that make it possible. AI is not a single technology—it's an ecosystem of interconnected disciplines, models, frameworks, and systems that work together to deliver intelligent outcomes.

This chapter breaks down the AI toolbox into its essential components and explains how each is used in retail—from the models that drive recommendations to the interfaces that interact with customers in real time.

2.1 – What Is Artificial Intelligence?

Artificial Intelligence (AI) refers to machines or software systems that can mimic cognitive functions like learning, reasoning, problem-solving, and decision-making. In retail, this means software that can:

- Recommend the right product

- Forecast demand

- Recognize a customer's face or voice

- Chat with customers

- Optimize inventory or delivery routes

- Detect fraudulent transactions

AI combines **data**, **algorithms**, and **feedback loops** to deliver increasingly smarter decisions.

2.2 – Machine Learning (ML)

Machine Learning is the backbone of modern AI.

It refers to algorithms that learn from data to make predictions or decisions without being explicitly programmed for each outcome.

Types of Machine Learning:

- **Supervised Learning**: Trained on labeled data to predict outcomes. *Example:* Predicting if a customer will buy based on browsing history.

- **Unsupervised Learning**: Finds hidden patterns or groupings in data. *Example:* Customer segmentation for marketing.

- **Reinforcement Learning**: Learns through reward-based feedback. *Example:* Dynamic pricing that adjusts based on buyer response.

Retail Use Cases:

- Sales forecasting

AI IN RETAIL INDUSTRY

- Product recommendations

- Price optimization

- Customer churn prediction

2.3 – Natural Language Processing (NLP)

NLP enables machines to understand, interpret, and respond to human language.

Applications in Retail:

- Chatbots and voice assistants

- Product search and filtering

- Sentiment analysis from reviews

- Auto-generating product descriptions

- Translating customer service queries

Tools & Libraries:

- SpaCy

- NLTK

- OpenAI GPT models

- Google Dialogflow

- Amazon Lex

2.4 – Computer Vision

Computer Vision enables AI systems to understand visual inputs like images and videos.

Applications:

- Facial recognition for VIP identification

- Detecting out-of-stock shelves

- Analyzing in-store customer traffic

- Product tagging via image upload

- Visual search ("show me similar shoes")

Retail Tools:

- Amazon Rekognition

- Google Cloud Vision

- OpenCV

- Custom object detection models with YOLO or TensorFlow

2.5 – Recommendation Engines

Recommendation systems drive a large percentage of e-commerce revenue.

Types of Recommendation Models:

- **Collaborative Filtering**: Based on what similar users bought.

- **Content-Based Filtering**: Based on product attributes (color, size, category).

- **Hybrid Systems**: Combine both for higher accuracy.

Advanced Approaches:

- Neural networks for deep personalization

- Session-based recommendations

- Context-aware suggestions (location, time of day, mood)

Retail Impact:
 Increases conversions, basket size, and retention.

2.6 – Predictive Analytics

Predictive analytics use past data to forecast future events.

Retail Use Cases:

- Demand forecasting

- Inventory planning

- Product returns prediction

- Customer lifetime value (CLV) estimation

- Price elasticity analysis

Common Algorithms:

- Regression

- Decision Trees

- Gradient Boosting (XGBoost, LightGBM)

- Time series forecasting (ARIMA, Prophet, LSTM)

2.7 – Generative AI

Generative AI creates new content from learned data.

Applications:

- Writing product descriptions

- Generating social media content

- Designing marketing creatives

- Producing chatbot replies

- Creating 3D product models or outfit simulations

Popular Tools:

- ChatGPT

- DALL·E

- Midjourney

- Jasper AI

- Copy.ai

2.8 – AI in Automation and RPA

Robotic Process Automation (RPA) combined with AI powers repetitive task automation.

Retail Applications:

- Invoice processing

- Email triaging

- Order confirmations

- Product catalog updates

- Loyalty points reconciliation

Tools:

- UiPath

- Automation Anywhere

- Blue Prism

2.9 – Sentiment and Emotion AI

These tools help retailers understand customer mood and feedback.

Sources of Input:

- Text reviews

- Voice tone

- Facial expressions

- Emojis and reactions on social

Applications:

- Product design feedback

- Emotional retargeting

- Customer satisfaction measurement

Tools:

- Affectiva

- Microsoft Text Analytics

- IBM Tone Analyzer

2.10 – Real-Time Analytics and Edge AI

Retail requires speed. **Edge AI** allows devices like kiosks, cameras, and POS systems to process data locally.

Use Cases:

- Instant inventory recognition

- Real-time fraud detection

- Smart signage that reacts to viewer demographics

- Checkout-free systems

Tools:

- NVIDIA Jetson

- AWS Greengrass

- Google Coral

2.11 – AI Platforms and APIs for Retail

Retailers don't always build AI from scratch. They use platforms and APIs.

Top AI Platforms:

- **Google Vertex AI**

- **Amazon SageMaker**

- **Microsoft Azure ML**

- **Salesforce Einstein**

- **Adobe Sensei**

These offer:

- No-code/low-code interfaces

- Model training environments

- Deployment pipelines

- Retail-specific APIs for personalization, forecasting, vision

2.12 – Data Infrastructure for AI

AI needs good data. Key components:

- **Data Lakes**: Store structured and unstructured data

- **ETL Pipelines**: Extract, transform, load data for models

- **Customer Data Platforms (CDPs)**: Centralize customer interactions

- **Data Warehouses**: Optimize queries and performance

- **Cloud Integration**: Access and scale AI globally

Without strong data plumbing, even the smartest AI fails.

2.13 – Integration with Legacy Systems

Most retailers have existing POS, ERP, and CRM systems. AI must **connect, not conflict**.

Solutions:

- API bridges

- Middleware platforms (e.g., MuleSoft, Zapier)

- Data virtualization tools

- AI microservices wrapping legacy functions

A hybrid approach helps legacy and modern systems coexist.

2.14 – Building vs. Buying AI

When to Build:

- You need competitive differentiation

- Your data is unique and valuable

- You have internal AI expertise

When to Buy:

- You need speed to market

- You're solving standard problems

- You lack in-house data science

Approach:
Start with buying, move toward building as your AI maturity grows.

2.15 – Conclusion: Assemble Your AI Toolbox

Every retailer—large or small—can benefit from the AI toolbox. You don't need to use everything at once. Start with a problem, match it to the right tool, test, and grow.

AI isn't about replacing your business—it's about **upgrading it intelligently**.

Chapter 3

Reinventing Customer Experience with AI

Customer experience has always been at the heart of retail. But in today's digital-first, hyper-personalized, always-on world, traditional methods of engaging customers are no longer enough. Consumers now expect experiences that are not just convenient but intelligent—experiences that remember, adapt, predict, and respond instantly.

AI doesn't just improve customer experience—it transforms it. By understanding behavior, context, emotion, and history, AI enables retailers to move from *generic service* to *precision engagement*, from *mass marketing* to *moments that matter*.

3.1 – The Evolving Customer Journey

The customer journey today is complex, nonlinear, and omnichannel. A buyer might:

- Browse online on Monday

- See an Instagram ad on Tuesday

- Visit a store on Friday

- Complete the purchase on Saturday via mobile

AI helps retailers map and optimize these journeys by:

- Capturing multi-touch behavior across channels

- Identifying bottlenecks or churn points

- Delivering interventions (e.g., cart reminders, support offers) at the right time

The goal is to **meet the customer where they are**—not where the brand wants them to be.

3.2 – AI-Powered Personalization in Action

Retail AI systems personalize:

- **Product recommendations** (based on behavior, season, geography)

- **Homepage content** (what's shown, what's hidden)

- **Promotions and discounts** (tailored to profile or purchase history)

- **Navigation flows** (what's prioritized based on user persona)

Example:
Netflix's homepage algorithm inspired e-commerce brands to show different layouts to different users—even if the product catalog is identical.

3.3 – Conversational AI: Chatbots and Virtual Assistants

Chatbots powered by NLP are now central to customer interaction.

Capabilities:

- Answer FAQs

- Recommend products

- Handle returns

- Provide order tracking

- Escalate to human agents

Voice AI assistants on smart speakers allow hands-free ordering, reordering, and support.

Benefits:

- 24/7 support

- Scalable customer service

- Instant response times

- High-quality interaction consistency

Example:
H&M's chatbot offers style advice based on user-selected looks and preferences.

3.4 – Sentiment Analysis and Emotion Recognition

AI detects tone and sentiment from:

- **Text**: Review polarity, chat anger detection

- **Voice**: Frustration in call center tone

- **Face**: In-store mood via camera

This allows retailers to:

- De-escalate in real time

- Trigger empathy-based messaging

- Refine product reviews and ratings

- Avoid sending offers to irritated customers

Example:
 AI flags a negative review with high influence potential, alerting customer service for personal outreach.

3.5 – Visual Search and Image-Based Discovery

Consumers often think visually. AI lets users:

- Upload a photo to find similar products

- Use camera scans to match in-store products

- Explore outfit combinations in AR

Tools:
Google Lens, Pinterest Lens, Snap Scan

Impact:
Increases discovery, reduces friction, and appeals to mobile-first generations.

3.6 – Virtual Try-Ons and Augmented Reality (AR)

Try-before-you-buy is now virtual.

Use Cases:

- Glasses (Warby Parker)

- Lipstick and foundation (Sephora, L'Oréal)

- Furniture placement (IKEA Place)

- Shoes and apparel (Nike Fit)

Technology Used:
Face tracking, AR overlays, motion detection

Result:
More confident purchases, reduced returns, and delightfully interactive experiences.

3.7 – Dynamic Content and UX

AI adjusts:

- Page layouts

- Hero banners

- Call-to-actions

- Checkout prompts

All based on:

- Device type

- Behavior history

- Demographics

- A/B test results

Goal: Create a flow that feels intuitive and personalized.

3.8 – Predictive Support and Proactive Service

AI anticipates needs before users ask:

- Auto-offers extended warranties at checkout

- Notifies when frequently bought items may run low

- Detects frustration in navigation and offers live support

- Suggests size up/down based on return history

Example:
Chewy uses AI to send personalized gifts and condolences for pet-related purchases—building emotional loyalty.

3.9 – Loyalty and Retention via AI

Smart loyalty platforms:

- Offer points dynamically based on CLV (customer lifetime value)

- Trigger retention campaigns before predicted churn

- Recommend next purchase to increase stickiness

- Combine online and offline behaviors into one profile

Example:
Starbucks AI tracks time-of-day behavior and sends targeted drink offers based on habit.

3.10 – Voice Commerce and Zero UI

Voice assistants are emerging as a new retail frontier.

Common Interactions:

- "Order more dog food"

- "Where is my package?"

- "Add socks to my cart"

- "Play product reviews for this camera"

Challenges:

- Need for clear structure in voice interactions

- Visual validation still required for complex decisions

Voice is best for reordering, support, and quick queries.

3.11 – Real-Time Response and Micro-Moments

AI enables fast reactions to user behavior.

- Bounce prevention with exit-intent offers

- Triggered recommendations after dwell time on a product

- Smart nudges ("You might like…") after a scroll pause

Each of these **micro-moments** can make or break the sale.

3.12 – Case Studies in CX Transformation

1. Sephora
Blends AI, AR, and beauty advisors to deliver hybrid shopping excellence.

2. Stitch Fix
Combines human stylists with machine learning recommendations to create a scalable yet personal experience.

3. Amazon
Master of anticipatory service—"People who bought this also bought…" is now a benchmark.

4. Alibaba
Deploys emotion-detection AI in fashion pop-ups to recommend items based on facial expressions.

3.13 – Measuring AI Impact on Experience

KPIs to Track:

- NPS (Net Promoter Score)

- CSAT (Customer Satisfaction)

- Conversion rate lift from recommendations

- Engagement time

- Bounce and churn rates

- Average order value (AOV)

Use A/B testing to validate every AI-powered experience before full rollout.

3.14 – Pitfalls to Avoid

- **Over-automation**: Bots that frustrate rather than help

- **Uncanny personalization**: Creepy rather than helpful

- **Inconsistent experiences across channels**

- **AI hallucinations** in generative responses

- **Bias in product exposure** (favoring high-margin over relevance)

Solution: Always keep **human judgment in the loop**.

3.15 – Conclusion: CX Is the Competitive Edge

In a world where products and prices are increasingly commoditized, **experience is the differentiator**. AI gives retailers the tools to create experiences that are faster, smarter, more personal, and emotionally resonant.

Customer loyalty is no longer won by discounts or branding alone—it's earned one intelligent moment at a time.

Chapter 4

Personalization: From Predictive Models to Emotional AI

Retail personalization has evolved from a marketing gimmick to a strategic necessity. Today's customers expect experiences that feel tailored just for them—across every touchpoint. AI enables retailers to deliver those experiences not just efficiently, but **intelligently and empathetically**.

In this chapter, we explore the full personalization spectrum: from machine learning models that predict buying behavior to emerging emotional AI that responds to a customer's mood. Personalization is no longer about names in emails—it's about **delivering relevance at the speed of thought**.

4.1 – Why Personalization Matters

- 80% of customers are more likely to buy from brands that offer personalized experiences

- 44% are likely to become repeat buyers after a tailored experience

- Personalization drives up to a **20% increase in revenue** for digital retailers

Modern consumers expect:

- Context-aware product suggestions

- Personalized promotions

- Adaptive navigation

- Real-time engagement

Without personalization, retailers risk irrelevance.

4.2 – The Evolution of Personalization

Phase 1: Demographic-Based

- "If female, show dresses"

- Static segmentation by age, gender, income

Phase 2: Behavior-Based

- "You bought X, so you may like Y"

- Browsing and purchase history analysis

Phase 3: Predictive Personalization

- AI models forecast needs and interests

- Offers tailored by CLV, timing, mood, channel

Phase 4: Hyper-Personalization

- Every page, product, message, and price is dynamically adjusted per user

Phase 5: Emotional AI

- Systems detect mood via text, tone, or face

- Experience adapts accordingly

4.3 – Core Components of AI Personalization

1. User Profiles
Built from browsing history, purchases, reviews, location, and behavior signals.

2. Recommendation Engines
ML models that match users to products or content.

3. Contextual Triggers
Time, weather, device, geography, session duration.

4. Content Adaptation
Dynamic UI elements change per user (banners, offers, product sort order).

5. Predictive Models
Estimate churn, basket size, offer acceptance, next best action.

4.4 – Types of Personalization in Retail

- **Product Recommendations**

- **Personalized Pricing and Offers**

- **Adaptive Navigation**

- **Customized Emails and SMS**

- **Smart Search Results**

- **Geo-Personalized Promotions**

- **Predictive Stock Alerts**

4.5 – AI Techniques Behind the Curtain

Collaborative Filtering
"Customers like you also liked…"—based on similar behavior patterns.

Content-Based Filtering
Matches items to user preferences based on attributes.

Hybrid Models
Combines collaborative and content-based for higher accuracy.

Deep Learning Models
Neural networks handle large-scale, high-dimensional personalization with excellent results.

Reinforcement Learning
Continuously improves through feedback and real-time behavior.

4.6 – Personalized Search and Merchandising

AI adjusts:

- Auto-suggestions as you type

- Search result order

- Filters shown by default

- In-stock and trending prioritization

- Visual search matching uploaded photos

Example:
 A shopper searching for "shoes" gets athletic sneakers prioritized, based on their previous clicks and cart items.

4.7 – Personalized Content and Pages

AI customizes:

- Homepage layout

- Banners

- Category order

- Call-to-actions

- Blog articles or guides based on past engagement

Example:
 A fashion site shows different top banners to a student versus a business professional—based on inferred persona.

4.8 – Personalized Promotions and Pricing

AI can:

- Offer unique coupon codes

- Trigger cart discounts at predicted churn points

- Show pricing adjusted for loyalty level or behavior

Caution:
Personalized pricing must remain transparent to avoid customer backlash.

4.9 – Loyalty and Retention Personalization

Personalization improves retention by:

- Predicting and preventing churn

- Suggesting points redemption

- Sending milestone rewards

- Offering next-step loyalty tiers

Example:
Amazon suggests items based on reorder frequency and notifies when it's time to replenish.

4.10 – Cross-Channel Personalization

Consistency is key.

AI syncs experiences across:

- Website

- Mobile apps

- Emails

- SMS

- Chatbots

- In-store tablets

Example:
A cart built on desktop appears in the mobile app. An in-store associate accesses recent wishlists via CRM.

4.11 – Emotional AI: The Next Frontier

AI is learning to **feel**.

Emotion AI uses:

- Facial recognition

- Voice sentiment

- Textual emotion detection

Applications:

- Calming tone if stress is detected

- Upbeat visuals for happy users

- Support escalation for frustration

Example:
A chatbot detecting irritation changes tone and fast-tracks human handoff.

4.12 – AI in Customer Segmentation

Traditional segments are static. AI creates **fluid micro-segments**:

- Fashion-forward budget buyers

- High-frequency but low-spend users

- Impulse buyers vs. planners

These personas evolve with behavior and are used to tailor messages, flows, and journeys.

4.13 – Generative Personalization

AI now generates:

- Personalized emails

- Dynamic landing pages

- Product bundles

- Fashion inspiration feeds

- AR try-on recommendations

Tools Used:
ChatGPT, Jasper, Adobe Firefly

4.14 – Ethics and Privacy in Personalization

Risks:

- Overreach (creepiness)

- Bias in product exposure

- Unfair dynamic pricing

- Lack of transparency

Best Practices:

- Provide opt-outs

- Clearly label personalized content

- Avoid targeting vulnerabilities (e.g., grief, illness)

- Rotate content to avoid filter bubbles

4.15 – KPIs to Track

- Click-through rate (CTR) on personalized offers

- Average order value (AOV)

- Churn rate

- Conversion lift per personalized segment

- Personalization engagement rate

- Time spent per session

Use A/B testing to validate personalization impact.

4.16 – Case Studies in Personalization

Amazon
Delivers 1:1 homepage, search, and promo experiences to millions using real-time personalization.

Spotify
Creates weekly music recommendations and custom playlists powered by deep learning.

Netflix
Personalizes not just shows—but thumbnails, categories, and order of presentation.

Nike
Uses foot scans, past purchases, and fitness data to recommend gear across app and in-store.

4.17 – Conclusion: Relevance Is the New Retail Currency

In the age of endless choice, the real luxury is **relevance**. AI personalization transforms commerce from transactional to relational. It turns each user into a segment of one—understood, anticipated, and remembered.

The retailers that win tomorrow are the ones who can say to every customer: "This is *just* for you"—and mean it.

Chapter 5

Inventory Intelligence: AI in Supply Chain Optimization

Inventory has long been a balancing act in retail. Stock too much, and you lose money in storage and markdowns. Stock too little, and you lose sales and customer trust. The old ways of managing inventory—seasonal projections, rule-of-thumb reorder points, and reactive restocking—no longer suffice in a world where speed, personalization, and omnichannel fulfillment are the norm.

Enter AI. Inventory intelligence powered by artificial intelligence transforms retail from **guesswork to precision**. This chapter explores how AI optimizes the entire inventory lifecycle—from forecasting and ordering to warehouse management, fulfillment, and returns.

5.1 – The Inventory Dilemma

Traditional inventory methods struggle with:

- Inaccurate demand predictions

- Overstock and markdown losses

- Stockouts and missed sales

- Siloed supply chain systems

- Manual restocking processes

- Long lead times from factory to floor

In an era of fast fashion, on-demand delivery, and global supply disruptions, **AI is no longer optional—it's essential.**

5.2 – Demand Forecasting with Machine Learning

AI-powered forecasting goes far beyond historical sales averages.

What it analyzes:

- Past sales (daily, weekly, seasonal trends)

- Customer behavior and intent

- Local events and weather

- Economic indicators and price sensitivity

- Social media trends and influencer impact

- Competitor activity

Models Used:

- Time-series forecasting (ARIMA, Prophet)

- Deep learning models (LSTM networks)

- Ensemble approaches blending ML and domain rules

Impact:
Improved forecast accuracy = reduced stockouts and less capital locked in inventory.

5.3 – Real-Time Replenishment

Traditional restocking was reactive. AI enables **proactive, real-time replenishment**.

How it works:

- Inventory levels are monitored continuously

- Sell-through velocity triggers auto-reorders

- Lead times and vendor constraints are factored in

- Promotions and seasonality are pre-modeled

Example:
 AI alerts that an item's rate of sale has doubled this week and auto-generates a replenishment order from the optimal supplier.

5.4 – Smart Inventory Classification

AI dynamically classifies products by:

- Sales velocity

- Gross margin

- Seasonality

- Elasticity

- Location-specific performance

This allows for:

- Strategic SKU rationalization

- Targeted promotions or markdowns

- Regional stock allocation

- Just-in-time replenishment for low-margin items

5.5 – AI in Warehouse Management

AI optimizes warehouse operations via:

- Slotting optimization: placing high-frequency SKUs closer to pick zones

- Robotic picking and packing

- Predictive stock movements

- Temperature control and shelf life tracking

- Workforce scheduling based on demand

Example:
Zara's smart warehouses track garments from cutting to folding to shipping with AI-guided automation.

5.6 – Shelf Monitoring and Computer Vision

Computer vision systems use cameras and sensors to monitor physical shelf stock.

Functions:

- Detect empty spaces

- Trigger restock alerts

- Confirm product placement compliance

- Track customer-shelf interaction

Retailers Using This:

- Walmart

- Amazon Fresh

- Walgreens

5.7 – Unified Inventory Visibility

Retailers need to see stock across:

- Stores

- Warehouses

- Third-party suppliers

- In-transit shipments

- Returns pipeline

AI integrates all sources into a real-time dashboard, enabling:

- Accurate "Available to Promise" (ATP)

- Cross-channel fulfillment (e.g., ship from store)

- Better click-and-collect accuracy

5.8 – Omnichannel Inventory Sync

In omnichannel retail, AI ensures:

- Online reflects real store inventory

- Store associates can access
  e-commerce orders

- Warehouse and vendor stock are
  shared

- Returns can be processed at any
  touchpoint

Outcome:
Customers never hear "Sorry, it's out of
stock"—when in fact it's in stock at another
node.

5.9 – Reverse Logistics and Returns Optimization

AI improves:

- Return prediction (who, what, when)

- Condition-based restocking

- Re-routing to correct warehouse or resale channel

- Fraud detection

- Personalized return offers to reduce churn

Example:
AI suggests an exchange rather than a refund based on user history and margin protection.

5.10 – Sustainability Through Smart Stocking

AI supports green retailing by:

- Reducing overproduction

- Avoiding waste through better expiry forecasting

- Optimizing shipping routes for carbon impact

- Enabling local fulfillment to cut emissions

- Predicting seasonal overstock for charity or resale redirection

5.11 – Integration with POS, ERP, and SCM Systems

AI doesn't replace existing systems—it enhances them.
 It integrates with:

- Point-of-Sale (POS)

- Enterprise Resource Planning (ERP)

- Supply Chain Management (SCM)

- Order Management Systems (OMS)

Result:
 Decision-making is faster, smarter, and more holistic.

5.12 – AI for Dynamic Safety Stock Levels

Traditional safety stock = fixed buffer.
AI safety stock = dynamic,
demand-sensitive buffer.

- Considers demand volatility

- Adapts to supplier reliability

- Reacts to current promotional uplift

- Updates daily, not monthly

Outcome:
Fewer outages, less capital lock-up.

5.13 – Real-Time Store Inventory Apps

In-store employees use AI apps to:

- Locate inventory instantly

- Recommend alternatives to out-of-stock items

- Reserve or redirect items

- Reorder in real time

- Optimize planograms and shelf layouts

Example:
Target associates use handheld devices powered by AI to manage stock, suggest substitutions, and fulfill pickups.

5.14 – Predictive Pricing and Markdown Optimization

Inventory holding cost impacts pricing strategy. AI helps decide:

- When to markdown

- By how much

- For which channel

- To which customer segment

Markdowns are no longer blunt instruments—they're surgical tools.

5.15 – Conclusion: Inventory as a Competitive Advantage

Inventory used to be a backend cost center. With AI, it becomes a **frontline strategic weapon**.

Retailers who master inventory intelligence can:

- Move faster than competitors

- Fulfill smarter than e-commerce giants

- Delight customers with consistent availability

- Reduce waste and increase sustainability

- Protect margins with predictive markdowns

In the AI age, your inventory isn't just what you have—it's **what you know** about what you have.

Chapter 6

Pricing, Demand, and Dynamic Market Models

Pricing is where strategy meets the customer's wallet. In retail, price isn't just a number—it's a signal. It reflects brand value, perceived quality, urgency, availability, and competitive positioning. But pricing has traditionally been reactive and rigid. With artificial intelligence, pricing becomes adaptive, personalized, and continuously optimized in real time.

This chapter explores how AI transforms retail pricing—from basic discounting and markdown management to dynamic models that respond to customer behavior, competitor activity, and broader market conditions.

6.1 – The High Stakes of Retail Pricing

Retail pricing impacts:

- **Revenue and profit margins**

- **Customer acquisition and retention**

- **Brand positioning**

- **Inventory turnover**

- **Competitor standing**

A small error in pricing strategy can cost millions. AI helps retailers price not just correctly—but *intelligently*.

6.2 – Traditional vs. AI-Driven Pricing

Traditional Pricing:

- Fixed markups over cost

- Monthly or quarterly price updates

- Manual markdowns and seasonal sales

- Same price for all shoppers

- Limited elasticity analysis

AI-Powered Pricing:

- Real-time adjustments based on demand, inventory, and competition

- Personalized pricing and promotions

- Elasticity modeling and prediction

- Dynamic bundling and upselling

- Hyperlocal pricing variations

6.3 – Core Elements of AI Pricing Systems

1. Data Ingestion

- Sales history

- Competitor prices

- Seasonality

- Inventory status

- Traffic data

- Promotions history

- External signals (weather, social trends)

2. Prediction Models

- Demand forecasting

- Elasticity modeling

- Conversion probability

- Price sensitivity scoring

3. Optimization Engine

- Maximizes revenue or margin

- Balances stock and customer value

- Simulates multiple price points

4. Testing and Feedback

- A/B testing

- Continuous learning from user behavior

- Price testing under varying conditions

6.4 – Dynamic Pricing in Retail

AI sets and adjusts prices dynamically across:

- Time of day

- Inventory levels

- Customer location or segment

- Competitor actions

- Cart contents or wish list behavior

- Season and holiday cycles

Example:
Flight and hotel prices change hourly based on AI-driven demand modeling. Retail is catching up fast.

6.5 – Personalized Pricing and Offers

AI customizes pricing or promotions for individuals or micro-segments.

Signals Used:

- Loyalty status

- Purchase history

- Browsing duration

- Cart behavior

- Predicted lifetime value (CLV)

Techniques:

- Rule-based tiers (gold, silver, bronze customers)

- Real-time scoring

- Next best offer (NBO) engines

Caution:
Personalized pricing must be **transparent and ethical** to avoid customer distrust.

6.6 – Markdown Optimization with AI

Markdowns are necessary to clear inventory, but often poorly timed.

AI solves:

- When to start discounting

- What depth is needed

- Which channels to target

- Who gets offers (vs. full-price buyers)

- Whether bundling is more effective than markdowns

Outcome:
Minimized margin loss, higher sell-through, and fewer liquidation costs.

6.7 – Price Elasticity Modeling

Elasticity = How sensitive demand is to price changes.

AI determines:

- Elastic vs. inelastic products

- Optimal price range for conversion

- Customer group response to pricing

- Cross-elasticity (how one product's price affects others)

Example:
 Raising the price of a popular T-shirt may reduce demand—but bundling it with a discount on jeans keeps the basket value stable.

6.8 – Competitor Price Monitoring and Response

AI scrapes competitor websites or third-party feeds to:

- Detect price drops or increases

- Adjust pricing rules automatically

- Protect margin floors

- Identify promotion timing patterns

- Adjust PPC bids dynamically

Tools Used:
Prisync, Intelligence Node, Omnia Retail

6.9 – Bundling and Upsell Optimization

AI identifies:

- Product affinities

- High-margin bundle opportunities

- Trigger points for cross-selling

- Dynamic offer timing (e.g., after add-to-cart)

Examples:

- "Buy 2, get 1 free" bundles personalized per user

- Dynamic bundles (e.g., shoes + socks) with real-time pricing changes

6.10 – Surge and Event-Based Pricing

AI responds to:

- Local events (concerts, sports, festivals)

- Demand spikes (weather, news coverage, influencer mentions)

- Limited-time offers or flash sales

Retailers now use AI to run **lightning discounts**, adjusting inventory and pricing live as behavior changes.

6.11 – Channel-Specific Pricing Strategies

AI sets different prices for:

- Mobile vs. desktop

- App vs. website

- In-store vs. online

- Geo-targeted offers by city or region

Example:
An item might be $29.99 on mobile (with a push notification offer), and $34.99 on desktop.

6.12 – Generative AI in Pricing Messaging

AI writes:

- Promotion headlines

- Price justification messaging

- Call-to-actions for sales

- Email subject lines and body copy

Impact:
Higher click-through and conversion rates when AI matches message tone to customer persona.

6.13 – Ethical Considerations in AI Pricing

Risks:

- Hidden dynamic pricing

- Algorithmic bias against certain locations or devices

- Manipulative urgency triggers

- Price gouging during emergencies

Best Practices:

- Disclose personalization policies

- Offer opt-outs

- Avoid discriminatory patterns

- Monitor for fairness and model drift

6.14 – Regulatory Environment

Regions like the EU and California enforce:

- Transparency around automated decisions

- Consent for price-based profiling

- Anti-discrimination protections

Retailers must prepare for:

- Algorithm audits

- Explainability in pricing

- Legal challenges if AI pricing harms competition or fairness

6.15 – KPIs to Track

- Price elasticity by product or category

- Promotion redemption rate

- Conversion rate per price tier

- Gross margin after discount

- Inventory velocity post-markdown

- Competitor price parity score

6.16 – Real-World Examples

Amazon
Runs millions of price changes per day using demand and competitor models.

Booking.com
Uses price testing and segmentation to optimize conversions by geography.

Walmart
Combines real-time pricing with supply chain analytics to maintain low prices with high availability.

Alibaba
Uses AI to predict optimal prices during massive events like Singles' Day.

6.17 – Conclusion: Price Meets Precision

AI empowers retailers to move beyond static pricing to **fluid, intelligent, and customer-aware pricing strategies**.

Retailers who master AI pricing will:

- Maximize profit margins

- Convert more customers

- Clear inventory faster

- Protect brand equity

- Stay ahead of price wars

In an AI-powered market, pricing is no longer just math—it's **strategy, psychology, and machine intelligence combined**.

Chapter 7

AI and the New Retail Workforce

Retail has always been a people-powered industry. From greeters and cashiers to merchandisers and store managers, human interaction was once the defining feature of retail. But with the rise of AI, automation, and intelligent systems, the nature of retail work is changing dramatically—not disappearing, but evolving.

This chapter explores how AI is reshaping retail roles, what new jobs are emerging, how employees are being empowered by technology, and how businesses can upskill their teams to thrive in a blended human-AI environment.

7.1 – Automation Anxiety vs. Augmentation Reality

The myth: AI will eliminate retail jobs.
The truth: AI will **augment** most jobs and create new ones.

Tasks being automated:

- Manual stock checks

- Invoice processing

- Basic customer support

- Inventory reconciliation

- Schedule planning

Tasks being enhanced:

- Personalized customer service

- Visual merchandising

- Store experience design

- Problem-solving and cross-selling

- Strategic planning

7.2 – Changing Roles in Retail

Store Associates now use AI tools to:

- Access customer preferences and purchase history

- Check real-time inventory across locations

- Suggest complementary products

- Process returns or exchanges instantly

- Upsell based on smart recommendations

Store Managers rely on AI for:

- Forecasting foot traffic

- Optimizing staff schedules

- Planning promotions

- Managing local assortments

Customer Service Agents use:

AI IN RETAIL INDUSTRY
120

- AI co-pilots to answer complex queries

- Real-time sentiment tracking

- Omnichannel communication dashboards

7.3 – New Jobs Created by AI in Retail

AI is also **creating entirely new roles** in retail:

1. **AI Trainer / Annotator**
   Prepares and labels data used to train AI systems (e.g., customer queries, product images).

2. **Retail Data Scientist**
   Builds models for demand forecasting, churn prediction, and dynamic pricing.

3. **AI Product Manager**
   Defines use cases, user stories, and performance metrics for AI-powered features.

4. **Conversational Experience Designer**
   Crafts chatbot scripts and virtual assistant flows with brand voice consistency.

5. **Ethical AI Advisor**
   Ensures transparency, fairness, and

compliance in AI deployment.

6. **Automation Workflow Architect**
   Designs robotic and AI-driven task flows for operations and customer support.

7.4 – Reskilling the Retail Workforce

Retailers must invest in **upskilling** and **reskilling** their employees to stay relevant in an AI-driven environment.

In-demand skills:

- Digital literacy (devices, dashboards, apps)

- Data literacy (interpreting and using analytics)

- Customer empathy and adaptive communication

- Basic AI and machine learning understanding

- Ethics and privacy awareness

Methods:

- Online learning platforms (e.g., Coursera, edX, Udemy)

- In-house training programs

- Cross-functional project exposure

- Certifications (Google AI, Microsoft Azure AI, Salesforce Einstein)

7.5 – AI-Powered Hiring and Talent Management

AI streamlines recruitment by:

- Scanning and scoring resumes

- Conducting video interviews with emotion analysis

- Predicting candidate fit and turnover risk

- Automating offer letters and onboarding

Ethical watchout: Bias in AI hiring tools must be monitored to avoid reinforcing discrimination.

AI also helps with:

- Performance management

- Identifying training needs

- Personalized learning paths

7.6 – Employee Empowerment via AI

AI gives frontline workers superpowers.
They can:

- Check inventory or place orders on mobile devices

- Suggest personalized offers via clienteling apps

- Handle customer issues faster with AI assistants

- View analytics to improve upselling performance

Example:
Sephora store advisors use tablets to pull up customer history and make real-time beauty recommendations.

7.7 – Collaborative Robots (Cobots) in Retail

Cobots are designed to work alongside humans.

Functions:

- Stock scanning

- Price checks

- Shelf organization

- In-store cleaning

- Assisting with curbside pickups

Retailers using cobots:
Walmart, Lowe's, Decathlon

Outcome:
 Frees up human staff for high-value, emotionally intelligent work.

7.8 – Gig Work and AI Scheduling Platforms

AI enables flexible staffing models by:

- Forecasting peak hours

- Matching available workers to shifts

- Balancing cost and coverage

- Providing mobile shift swaps and self-service apps

Platforms:
ShiftSmart, Instawork, Qwick

Impact:
Improved labor efficiency and worker satisfaction.

7.9 – Performance Analytics and Coaching

AI tracks and supports employee performance by:

- Monitoring service quality

- Detecting tone and sentiment in calls

- Suggesting next-best-actions

- Recommending coaching based on behavior gaps

Concerns:
Avoid using AI as a surveillance tool—focus on empowerment, not micromanagement.

7.10 – Building a Human-Centered AI Culture

For AI to succeed, **people must believe in it.**

Best Practices:

- Involve employees early in AI pilot projects

- Share AI benefits and success stories

- Provide transparency about data use

- Design tools with frontline input

- Celebrate human wins enabled by AI

Cultural principles:

- AI supports, not replaces

- Every employee is an innovator

- Digital skills are everyone's responsibility

7.11 – The Role of Leadership

Retail leaders must:

- Champion AI as a force for good

- Invest in workforce transformation

- Set ethical standards for AI use

- Encourage experimentation

- Reward learning and adaptability

AI success is a leadership issue—not just a technology one.

7.12 – Future of Work in Retail

Hybrid Teams: Humans + Machines
Fluid Careers: From merchandiser to data-driven experience manager
Soft Skill Dominance: Empathy, storytelling, and ethics rise in value
Global Talent Pools: Remote AI teams driving personalization and analytics
Lifelong Learning: Continuous skill refresh becomes the norm

7.13 – Conclusion: Humans at the Center of AI

AI is transforming retail roles—but not replacing people. Instead, it's making them **smarter, faster, more creative, and more effective**.

The future belongs to retailers who invest in both **intelligent machines and empowered humans**—because technology may power the engine, but it's people who steer the experience.

Chapter 8

From Brick to Click: Omnichannel Excellence with AI

Retail has always been about being where the customer is. But in today's world, the customer is everywhere—on mobile, in-store, on social media, on smart speakers, and across marketplaces. The challenge is not simply to be present on all these channels, but to connect them into a single, unified journey.

This chapter explores how AI enables **omnichannel retail**—a seamless fusion of physical and digital touchpoints powered by intelligent systems that recognize customers, personalize experiences, and optimize logistics in real time.

8.1 – What Is Omnichannel Retail?

Multichannel means offering multiple shopping platforms.
 Omnichannel means integrating them so the customer journey feels continuous and coherent.

Omnichannel involves:

- Unified inventory across store, online, mobile

- Shared customer profiles across systems

- Consistent promotions and offers

- Flexible fulfillment (e.g., buy online, pick up in-store)

- Data flowing between every touchpoint

Goal: Treat every channel as part of one relationship—not a siloed experience.

8.2 – The Role of AI in Omnichannel

AI makes omnichannel retail **intelligent** by:

- Recognizing shoppers across devices and stores

- Predicting what they want next

- Recommending the best channel for engagement

- Routing orders dynamically

- Analyzing cross-channel journeys in real time

Without AI, omnichannel is a **logistics headache**. With AI, it becomes a **symphony of personalization**.

8.3 – Customer Identity Resolution

AI connects the dots between:

- Guest checkouts

- Loyalty logins

- Email interactions

- Mobile app usage

- Store visits and POS data

- Social media behavior

Result: A **unified customer profile**—the foundation for consistent, personalized experiences.

8.4 – Personalized Journeys Across Channels

AI powers:

- **Email product suggestions** based on in-app browsing

- **Mobile push notifications** based on in-store visits

- **Store kiosks** that pull up online wish lists

- **Website banners** based on purchase history

Example:
A shopper adds sneakers to their cart on desktop but doesn't check out. The next day, they receive a mobile push offer for the same item—available at a nearby store.

8.5 – Real-Time Inventory Visibility

AI aggregates inventory across:

- Warehouses

- Stores

- Dropship vendors

- In-transit shipments

Customer sees:

- Accurate "in stock" messages

- Delivery time estimates

- Local store availability

- Alternative pickup locations

Employee sees:

- Unified order dashboard

- Smart replenishment alerts

- Demand forecasts per location

8.6 – AI in Omnichannel Fulfillment

AI routes each order to the **best fulfillment source**:

- Closest warehouse with stock

- Store nearest to customer

- Vendor partner for direct shipping

- Consolidated orders to reduce cost

Optimizes for:

- Speed

- Cost

- Carbon footprint

- Customer preference

Use Case:
"Ship from store" models powered by AI reduce delivery time and unlock store inventory for online shoppers.

8.7 – Click-and-Collect and Curbside AI

AI enables:

- Real-time order readiness tracking

- Predictive arrival estimation

- Optimized store pick paths for staff

- Instant updates to customers

- Smart lockers and automated handoffs

Impact:
Faster pickups, higher NPS, and less staff stress.

8.8 – In-Store Digital and Smart Kiosks

AI enhances physical retail via:

- Interactive displays showing customer history

- Product recommendation engines

- Smart mirrors and AR experiences

- Contactless checkout stations

- Self-service personalization tools

Example:
 Nike stores let customers scan their app to unlock reserved products or get AI-powered fit advice.

8.9 – Social Commerce and Shoppable Content

AI helps brands sell via:

- Instagram

- TikTok

- YouTube

- Pinterest

- Facebook Marketplace

Functions:

- Identifying influencers and UGC trends

- Auto-generating ad creatives

- Matching content to inventory

- Personalizing feed ads

Tools:
Meta AI Ads, TikTok for Business,
Smartly.io, Dash Hudson

8.10 – Omnichannel Customer Support

AI connects support experiences across:

- Chatbots

- SMS

- Email

- Social messaging (WhatsApp, Messenger)

- Call centers

Goal: Ensure every support interaction has **full context**, regardless of where it starts or ends.

Example:
 A chatbot that fails to resolve an issue on Instagram escalates it to a human via email—with full conversation history intact.

8.11 – AI in Returns and Reverse Logistics

AI reduces the pain of omnichannel returns:

- Predicts which items are likely to be returned

- Recommends exchanges or credits instead

- Guides customers to nearest return points

- Optimizes refund timing and fraud detection

- Reintegrates inventory in real time

Result:
 Lower costs, faster restocking, better retention.

8.12 – Unified Analytics and Attribution

AI tracks:

- Customer journey across devices and channels

- Attribution of marketing spend (e.g., did the ad drive store visit?)

- ROI per channel and campaign

- Cross-channel engagement patterns

Tools:
Google Analytics 4, Amplitude, Segment, Bloomreach

8.13 – Case Studies in AI Omnichannel

1. Target

- Unified app and store experiences

- Drive Up service uses AI to track order prep and pickup

- Loyalty, offers, and inventory synced everywhere

2. Nordstrom

- Omnichannel personalization engine

- In-store stylists access online preferences

- Smart dressing room experiences

3. Alibaba

- Hema stores offer online-to-offline (O2O) grocery shopping

- AI routes 30-minute delivery based on location and traffic

8.14 – Challenges in Omnichannel AI

- Fragmented data systems

- Channel conflicts (store vs. online ownership)

- Disjointed user experience

- Lack of real-time inventory integration

- Privacy compliance across regions

Solutions:

- Invest in CDP (Customer Data Platform)

- Streamline tech stack

- Set cross-functional goals

- Prioritize seamless over siloed

8.15 – Conclusion: Unify or Be Forgotten

Customers don't think in channels—they think in **moments**.

Retailers who unify digital and physical experiences using AI will create journeys that are frictionless, intuitive, and personalized. Those who stay siloed will frustrate customers and lose relevance.

Omnichannel powered by AI is no longer a competitive edge—it's the **minimum expectation** in modern retail.

Chapter 9

Ethics, Privacy, and Trust in AI Retail Systems

Artificial Intelligence offers retail unprecedented power to personalize, predict, and optimize. But with that power comes great responsibility. As retailers deploy increasingly intelligent systems, questions around fairness, transparency, and privacy become central. Trust is now a **strategic asset**—and a fragile one.

This chapter explores how to build and sustain ethical AI systems in retail. We'll cover data privacy, algorithmic bias, consent, explainability, and the growing regulatory landscape.

9.1 – The Trust Imperative in Retail AI

Trust drives:

- Customer retention

- Brand reputation

- Regulatory compliance

- Shareholder confidence

AI without trust = risk.
 A single scandal over data misuse or price discrimination can cost millions in lost sales and damage.

9.2 – Three Pillars of Responsible AI

1. Fairness

- Avoid bias in product exposure, offers, or hiring

- Ensure equitable access across demographics

- Design for inclusivity (e.g., screen readers, multi-lingual chatbots)

2. Transparency

- Disclose when AI is used

- Provide explanations for key decisions

- Let users view or adjust personalization settings

3. Privacy

- Respect data ownership

- Collect only what's necessary

- Offer deletion and opt-out options

9.3 – Data Privacy and Customer Consent

Retail AI depends on data—but must treat it with respect.

Best Practices:

- Explicit consent for tracking and personalization

- Clear privacy policies in simple language

- Cookie management and opt-outs

- Data minimization (collect only what's needed)

- Periodic re-consent prompts

Example:
 A loyalty app asks for location access only when using "find nearest store"—not constantly in the background.

9.4 – GDPR, CCPA, and Global Regulations

Retailers must comply with:

- **GDPR (EU)**: Right to be forgotten, consent, explainability

- **CCPA (California)**: Right to know, delete, and opt out of data sales

- **Brazil LGPD, India's DPDP, China's PIPL**: All impose varying consent, storage, and use restrictions

Trend:
Laws are converging toward stricter, user-centric data ethics.

9.5 – Algorithmic Bias and Discrimination

AI models may unintentionally favor:

- Wealthy ZIP codes

- Predominantly male or white users

- Specific device types (iOS vs. Android)

- Certain physical appearances (in vision systems)

Risks:

- Unequal access to offers

- Discriminatory pricing

- Biased hiring or credit decisions

Solutions:

- Diverse training data

- Bias audits

- Fairness metrics

- Regular model retraining with feedback loops

9.6 – Explainable AI (XAI) in Retail

Black-box models are risky, especially in pricing and hiring.

XAI tools provide:

- Feature importance scores

- Visual explanations of recommendations

- Natural-language model summaries

- Decision pathway visualization

Use Cases:

- "Why was this price shown?"

- "How was this product recommended?"

- "Why was my return denied?"

9.7 – Responsible Personalization

Personalization becomes creepy when:

- It's too specific ("Hey Sarah, still want those red stilettos?")

- It exploits vulnerability (e.g., grief, illness)

- It feels manipulative (fake urgency or scarcity)

Responsible AI:

- Personalizes for relevance—not manipulation

- Offers control: "Show me less like this"

- Surfaces diverse content to avoid filter bubbles

9.8 – Security and Data Protection

AI models must be secured against:

- Data breaches

- Injection attacks (malicious inputs)

- Identity spoofing

- Unauthorized model use or resale

Best Practices:

- Encrypt sensitive data

- Use secure APIs

- Monitor model drift and inputs

- Anonymize wherever possible

9.9 – Ethical AI in Retail Hiring

AI hiring tools can:

- Screen resumes

- Score video interviews

- Recommend roles

Concerns:

- Penalizing gaps due to caregiving

- Preferring certain accents or facial structures

- Training on biased historical hiring data

Fixes:

- Human oversight

- Bias detection tools

- Diverse training data

- Applicant appeal process

9.10 – Green AI and Sustainability Ethics

Retailers must consider:

- Energy use of training large AI models

- E-waste from smart devices

- Supply chain transparency (AI to detect labor violations)

Trend:
 Green AI principles emphasize efficient, ethical, and environmentally sustainable machine learning.

9.11 – Labeling and Disclosure

Shoppers should know:

- When they're interacting with AI

- What data is being collected

- How it's used

- What options they have to control or erase it

Example:
Chatbots introduce themselves: "Hi, I'm an AI assistant. I can help with…"
Or: "These recommendations are generated by AI. Adjust your preferences here."

9.12 – Organizational AI Governance

Who should oversee AI ethics?

- Data Privacy Officers

- AI Ethics Committees

- External watchdogs and advisors

- Cross-functional review boards

Principles to adopt:

- AI Bill of Rights

- Ethical AI checklists before launch

- Impact assessments (social, legal, cultural)

9.13 – AI Trust as a Brand Differentiator

Brands can stand out by:

- Publishing AI principles

- Offering user dashboards with transparency controls

- Earning "Ethical AI" or "Trustworthy Tech" certifications

- Using AI not just for profit—but for purpose (e.g., inclusive sizing, accessibility, sustainability)

9.14 – Crisis Management and PR Preparedness

What happens when:

- A model shows bias

- Personal data leaks

- Pricing feels exploitative

Your crisis plan should include:

- Transparency and speed of communication

- Immediate customer recourse channels

- Internal accountability reviews

- Public commitment to improvement

9.15 – Conclusion: Trust Is the True Currency

AI is retail's rocket fuel—but trust is the oxygen. Without ethical foundations, even the most advanced AI systems can backfire.

Retailers who build **transparent, fair, secure, and customer-centric** AI systems will not only avoid risk—they will gain loyalty, differentiation, and long-term success.

AI will shape the future of retail—but ethics will shape the future of AI.

Chapter 10

The Future Store: AI, Robotics, and Immersive Commerce

The store of the future is not a distant dream—it is happening now. Retailers are reimagining their physical spaces to incorporate AI, robotics, and immersive technologies. These intelligent systems are making stores smarter, more responsive, and more engaging for customers than ever before.

This chapter explores how AI and emerging technologies are shaping the **future of physical retail**, from checkout-free shopping to in-store robots, virtual fitting rooms, and beyond.

10.1 – Redefining the Physical Store

The traditional brick-and-mortar store is evolving. What was once just a place for transactions is now a **dynamic experience hub**. In the future, stores will not simply house products—they will act as **smart spaces** that enhance the shopping journey and deepen customer engagement.

Key Features of the Future Store:

- AI-powered customer recognition

- Interactive displays and smart signage

- Voice-activated services

- Personalized experiences based on behavior

- Integration with mobile apps, IoT, and AR/VR

The future store is **alive** with data, continuously adjusting its offerings based on

customer preferences, stock levels, and
real-time behaviors.

10.2 – AI-Powered Store Infrastructure

AI is the backbone of the smart store, enhancing everything from layout to logistics. Here's how AI is embedded into the infrastructure:

- **Smart Shelves**: Sensors track inventory levels, automatically ordering new stock when it's low.

- **AI-Powered Lighting**: Intelligent lighting adjusts to the time of day or store traffic, creating an optimal shopping atmosphere.

- **Sensor-Driven Displays**: Digital displays respond to customer proximity, offering personalized content based on behavior.

- **Robotic Cleaning**: Robots autonomously clean floors, ensuring stores are always neat without human intervention.

Example:
At a leading electronics retailer, AI

AI IN RETAIL INDUSTRY

algorithms guide customers through the store via mobile apps, providing product information and promotions along the way.

10.3 – The Role of Robotics in Retail

Robots are no longer a futuristic novelty—they are practical, everyday tools enhancing retail operations.

Types of Robots in Retail:

- **Inventory Robots**: Automate stock counting and shelf scanning to ensure real-time accuracy.

- **Delivery Robots**: Autonomous robots handle last-mile delivery for in-store purchases or online orders.

- **Customer Interaction Robots**: Greet customers, offer product suggestions, and assist with checkout.

- **Warehouse Robots**: Speed up fulfillment processes with autonomous picking and sorting.

Example:
Walmart uses robots in stores to scan shelves for out-of-stock products, ensuring

customers always have access to what they
need.

10.4 – Immersive Experiences with AR/VR

Augmented Reality (AR) and Virtual Reality (VR) are revolutionizing how customers experience products.

- **AR Try-Ons**: Customers can virtually try on makeup, glasses, or clothing using their smartphones or in-store AR mirrors.

- **VR Showrooms**: Customers can walk through fully immersive virtual stores, viewing products in detail without visiting the physical location.

- **Interactive Displays**: Product information, videos, and customer reviews can be viewed via AR when pointing a phone at a product.

Example:
Sephora uses AR to allow customers to try on makeup virtually, improving conversion rates and customer satisfaction by providing a more personalized shopping experience.

10.5 – Checkout-Free Retail: The AI-Driven Future

AI is making traditional checkouts obsolete. In the future store, customers will walk in, pick up items, and leave without waiting in line. Here's how it works:

- **Smart Cameras and Sensors**: These track the items a customer picks up and adds them to a virtual cart.

- **Mobile App Integration**: The customer's mobile app automatically detects the items in their cart and charges them once they leave the store.

- **No Cashiers**: Payment is processed automatically via the app, eliminating the need for checkout lanes.

Example:
Amazon Go pioneered checkout-free retail. Shoppers enter the store, grab what they need, and simply walk out. The system automatically charges their Amazon account, with no cashiers or lines involved.

10.6 – Personalization at the Point of Sale

In-store personalization goes beyond promotions—it's about creating an experience that feels unique to each shopper.

How AI Enhances In-Store Personalization:

- **Facial Recognition**: Identifies loyal customers and shows them personalized offers upon entry.

- **Behavioral Tracking**: Recognizes customer preferences based on their past shopping behavior, triggering product recommendations or discounts.

- **Location-Based Offers**: Sends special offers when customers are near certain aisles or products in-store.

Example:
 When a loyal customer enters a store, the system may recognize them and offer a

personalized discount on items they've purchased before, improving customer loyalty and increasing sales.

10.7 – Smart Fitting Rooms: The AI Dressing Room

Fitting rooms are evolving with AI and AR to enhance the shopping experience.

- **Virtual Try-Ons**: AI-powered mirrors allow customers to see how clothes will look on them without trying them on physically.

- **Smart Mirrors**: Offer recommendations for accessories or other clothing items based on the current selection.

- **Stock Check**: If the item a customer wants isn't available in their size, smart mirrors can check availability in other stores or suggest alternatives.

Example:
Rebecca Minkoff's flagship stores feature smart fitting rooms where customers can browse additional colors and sizes from a touchscreen inside the room, and even ask for assistance via the mirror.

10.8 – Seamless Omnichannel Integration

The future store must connect seamlessly with online platforms to provide a true omnichannel experience.

- **Click-and-Collect**: Buy online and pick up in-store. AI-driven systems ensure the right products are ready for pickup at the right time.

- **Ship-from-Store**: For items not available in a customer's local store, AI dynamically routes orders from nearby locations.

- **Unified Customer Profiles**: Shoppers can access their purchase history, loyalty points, and preferences across both online and physical stores.

Example:
Target's mobile app allows customers to see what's available at local stores, select items for in-store pickup, and track their order status in real-time.

10.9 – In-Store Digital Assistants and Kiosks

AI-driven kiosks and assistants are becoming standard features in retail.

- **In-Store Navigation**: Kiosks help customers find products, suggest related items, and check stock availability.

- **Customer Service**: AI-powered assistants answer questions, help with returns, and even offer product demos.

- **Interactive Displays**: Touchscreens provide detailed information, reviews, and related product suggestions.

Example:
Best Buy uses kiosks where customers can interact with an AI assistant to compare products, check prices, and access special promotions.

10.10 – Data-Driven Store Design

AI is also transforming the physical design of stores. Smart systems gather data on:

- **Customer Flow**: AI tracks movement patterns to optimize store layouts, placing high-demand items in prime locations.

- **Shelf Optimization**: AI monitors stock and customer interactions with shelves, ensuring the most popular products are always in view and in-stock.

- **Dynamic Displays**: Based on foot traffic and customer behavior, stores can adjust digital signage or physical product displays.

Example:
IKEA uses AI to adjust its store layout based on real-time shopper behavior and feedback, ensuring popular items are always in prime spots.

10.11 – Sustainability in the Future Store

As AI makes stores more efficient, it also helps reduce their environmental impact:

- **Energy Optimization**: AI systems manage heating, cooling, and lighting based on store traffic and time of day.

- **Waste Reduction**: Predictive systems ensure stores don't over-order perishable goods, reducing food waste.

- **Smart Packaging**: AI can suggest eco-friendly packaging options and reduce waste in the shipping process.

Example:
 IKEA is reducing its carbon footprint by optimizing store energy use and packaging waste through AI-powered systems.

10.12 – The Challenges Ahead

Despite the exciting possibilities, there are still significant challenges in realizing the future store:

- **High Implementation Costs**: The technology required for AI, robotics, and immersive experiences can be expensive to implement at scale.

- **Data Privacy Concerns**: With customer data being used to power personalization, retailers must ensure they're transparent about data usage and compliant with privacy laws.

- **Technical Integration**: Legacy systems must be upgraded to support AI, which can be a complex and time-consuming process.

10.13 – Conclusion: A New Era for Retail

The future store is not about replacing the human touch—it's about **augmenting** it. AI, robotics, and immersive technologies create spaces where technology works in harmony with human interaction to offer a **smarter, more efficient, and more personalized** experience.

The stores of tomorrow are here today, and those retailers who embrace these innovations will lead the charge in the next era of retail.

Chapter 11

Startups, Case Studies & Retail AI Disruptors

The retail AI revolution isn't just driven by giants like Amazon or Walmart—it's also being powered by startups, direct-to-consumer (DTC) disruptors, and agile tech innovators who are building AI into the core of their business models. These new players are using artificial intelligence not as an add-on, but as a **strategic foundation**.

In this chapter, we dive into real-world case studies, explore emerging startups, and highlight how legacy brands are partnering with or learning from AI-native companies.

11.1 – Why Startups Win at AI

Startups often outperform legacy retailers in AI innovation because they:

- Start with **clean data stacks**

- Have **no legacy systems to maintain**

- Prioritize **experimentation over perfection**

- Embrace **cloud-native and API-first architectures**

- Attract AI-savvy, entrepreneurial talent

By focusing on niche problems and scaling fast, startups often set the innovation agenda—even for billion-dollar brands.

11.2 – Disruptive Startups Using AI in Retail

1. Stitch Fix

- Combines human stylists with AI to deliver personalized clothing boxes.

- Machine learning recommends styles, sizes, and fits based on user feedback and preferences.

2. Zippin

- Offers checkout-free technology to small retailers using computer vision and shelf sensors.

- Competes with Amazon Go by licensing technology to third-party stores.

3. Vue.ai

- Uses computer vision to automate product tagging, personalization, and search across fashion retailers.

4. Lily AI

- Translates emotional consumer language ("boho chic dress for beach") into structured taxonomy for product discovery.

5. Trigo

- Partners with grocery stores to build frictionless, AI-powered shopping experiences with autonomous checkout.

11.3 – Direct-to-Consumer (DTC) Brands Leading with AI

1. Warby Parker

- Uses AI for virtual try-ons, prescription checking, and face shape recommendations for glasses.

2. Glossier

- Builds products based on AI-analyzed customer feedback from social and community platforms.

3. Allbirds

- Forecasts demand using machine learning to reduce overproduction and align inventory with sustainability goals.

4. Casper

- AI chatbots act as sleep consultants, offering product suggestions based on lifestyle and sleep data.

11.4 – Global AI-Driven Retail Innovators

1. Tokopedia (Indonesia)

- Uses AI to recommend products, detect fraud, and personalize homepages in real time.

2. ShopUp (Bangladesh)

- Offers micro-merchants AI-powered tools for inventory management, finance, and logistics.

3. Jumia (Africa)

- Implements AI personalization across low-bandwidth environments with high regional diversity.

4. Fynd (India)

- Connects offline fashion inventory to online discovery using AI-based stock visibility and demand prediction.

11.5 – Incubators and Innovation Labs

Established retailers are investing in startups through:

- **Retail accelerators** (Target Takeoff, LVMH's Maison des Startups)

- **Corporate venture arms** (Walmart Global Tech, Unilever Ventures)

- **University research partnerships**

- **Hackathons and challenge grants** for AI-powered ideas

These collaborations allow large companies to pilot cutting-edge ideas without bearing the full risk of innovation.

11.6 – Case Study: Amazon

Amazon remains the benchmark for AI in retail:

- **Product Recommendations**: Drive over 35% of total sales.

- **Voice Commerce**: Alexa enables shopping, tracking, and reordering.

- **Amazon Go**: Checkout-free physical stores powered by computer vision.

- **Warehouse Automation**: AI directs robots for picking, sorting, and fulfillment.

- **Cloud Platform**: AWS provides AI tools (Forecast, Personalize, Rekognition) to other retailers.

11.7 – Case Study: Alibaba & Hema Stores

Alibaba coined the term **"New Retail"**—fusing online, offline, logistics, and data.

Hema supermarkets:

- Customers scan and shop with an app

- AI routes deliveries within 30 minutes

- Dynamic pricing adjusts to supply and demand

- Facial recognition enables cashless checkout

Alibaba's model turns physical stores into data-driven warehouses and customer experience hubs.

11.8 – Case Study: Walmart

Walmart has rapidly transformed into an AI-powered retailer:

- **Shelf Scanning Robots** detect stockouts and misplaced items.

- **Intelligent Scheduling** optimizes labor costs and availability.

- **Smart Pricing** adjusts products based on competition and demand.

- **Walmart Labs** develops in-house AI for search, personalization, and fulfillment.

- **Luminate Platform** shares retail analytics and insights with suppliers.

11.9 – Case Study: Sephora

Sephora uses AI to blend beauty and technology:

- **ModiFace** enables AR-powered virtual makeup try-ons.

- **Color IQ** scans customer skin tones for personalized foundation matches.

- **AI Chatbots** provide beauty consultations and product discovery.

- **Data-Driven Loyalty** tracks behavior and suggests personalized perks.

Sephora's innovation centers focus on creating **emotionally resonant tech experiences**.

11.10 – Lessons from AI Disruptors

1. **Start with one problem.** Solve it well, then scale.

2. **Make data the foundation.** Build around clean, centralized data.

3. **Use feedback loops.** Let the product learn and adapt from behavior.

4. **Design mobile-first.** Most customers live on their phones.

5. **Human + AI.** Don't replace people—augment them.

6. **Embed ethics early.** Design AI that protects user rights from the start.

11.11 – Startup Challenges

Even AI startups face hurdles:

- Cold start problem (no historical data)

- Customer acquisition costs

- Scaling algorithms to multiple product categories

- Integration with legacy retailers

- Balancing ethics with aggressive growth

Solution: Focus on solving a painful, measurable problem—not just being "AI-powered."

11.12 – The Corporate Disruptor Playbook

Enterprises can adapt startup practices by:

- Creating **in-house AI innovation hubs**

- Launching **skunkworks projects** outside of rigid processes

- Encouraging **cross-functional AI teams**

- Developing **internal AI product managers**

- Building **data lakes and real-time feedback systems**

11.13 – The Future of Retail AI Startups

Emerging trends include:

- **Synthetic Media**: AI-generated product photos, models, and demos

- **Emotion-Based Targeting**: Ads that respond to mood or tone

- **Predictive Visual Search**: Suggesting items before users search

- **Voice Shopping Platforms**: Fully conversational commerce

- **Decentralized Retail Models**: AI-powered micro-fulfillment via local vendors

Startups that can anticipate and build for these trends will lead the next decade of retail.

11.14 – Conclusion: Disruption Is the New Normal

The future of retail is **not just omnichannel—it's omnibrain**. Every store, every app, every interaction is an opportunity for intelligence.

Retailers who wait for perfection will be disrupted by those who start, test, and learn fast. Whether you're a legacy brand or a new entrant, success in AI-powered retail will come from your ability to **act like a startup—even if you're not one.**

Chapter 12

Your Path Ahead: AI Retail Careers & Business Integration

Artificial intelligence isn't just reshaping products, services, and customer experiences—it's reshaping careers. In the evolving world of retail, those who understand how to work with AI, build with it, or lead through it will become the future's most valuable talent. This chapter is your roadmap to personal and organizational growth in the AI-driven retail ecosystem.

Whether you're a sales associate, store manager, marketer, data analyst, or entrepreneur, there is a place for you in AI retail—if you're willing to learn, adapt, and lead.

12.1 – Careers in AI-Powered Retail

Emerging Roles:

- **Retail Data Analyst**: Deciphers data to find insights on customer behavior, sales trends, and inventory efficiency.

- **AI Product Manager**: Builds and deploys AI-powered features, from recommendation engines to chatbots.

- **Automation Engineer**: Designs robotic systems for fulfillment, checkout, and warehouse management.

- **AI Trainer / Annotator**: Prepares labeled datasets to train AI models.

- **Conversational UX Designer**: Crafts AI chatbot scripts and interfaces.

- **Ethics & Privacy Officer**: Ensures compliance and fair use of AI technologies.

Hybrid Careers:
Traditional roles like merchandisers, buyers, and store managers are evolving into hybrid functions that mix business acumen with tech fluency.

12.2 – Career Paths by Background

Sales & Customer Service:

- Learn AI clienteling tools

- Use dashboards to personalize interactions

- Upskill in omnichannel platforms and analytics

Marketing & Loyalty:

- Dive into CRM automation, segmentation, and predictive targeting

- Use AI tools to generate content and test campaigns

Merchandising & Buying:

- Analyze AI-generated trend forecasts

- Use smart planning and allocation tools

- Optimize product bundles and markdowns with data

Supply Chain & Logistics:

- Deploy demand forecasting models

- Integrate smart fulfillment and last-mile delivery AI

Technology & Data:

- Build NLP, vision, or recommendation models

- Manage AI pipelines and MLOps

- Ensure data compliance and ethical implementation

12.3 – Skills to Succeed in AI Retail

Technical Skills:

- Python, SQL, Tableau

- ML basics (classification, regression, clustering)

- Data wrangling and visualization

- APIs and automation tools

Business Skills:

- Customer journey mapping

- Experimentation and A/B testing

- ROI analysis of AI tools

- Agile product development

Soft Skills:

- Adaptability

- Communication across functions

- Critical thinking and ethical judgment

- Creativity in problem-solving

12.4 – Learning Resources and Certifications

Online Platforms:

- Coursera: AI for Everyone (Andrew Ng), AI in Business

- edX: Harvard Retail Management + AI tracks

- LinkedIn Learning: Retail Analytics, AI for Marketers

- Google AI, Microsoft Learn, IBM Applied AI

Certifications:

- AWS Certified Machine Learning

- Salesforce Einstein Certification

- Microsoft AI Fundamentals

- NVIDIA Deep Learning Certificate

Bootcamps & Workshops:

- General Assembly

- BrainStation

- Udacity Nanodegrees (AI for Business)

12.5 – Building an AI-Savvy Organization

For Leaders and Executives:

1. **Audit your capabilities**

   - Where is AI already used?

   - What data do you have?

2. **Create a cross-functional AI team**

   - Include IT, marketing, operations, and store teams.

3. **Start small, win early**

   - Pilot projects in personalization, pricing, or forecasting.

4. **Invest in data infrastructure**

   - Clean data > fancy models.

5. **Upskill everyone**

- Offer AI fluency training to all levels.

12.6 – Common Pitfalls in Adoption

- **Buying tools without a clear problem**

- **Over-automating and alienating staff/customers**

- **Letting IT own AI in isolation from business teams**

- **Ignoring change management and training needs**

- **Forgetting the importance of ethics, bias, and transparency**

12.7 – The AI Innovation Loop

1. **Collect Data**

2. **Analyze for insights**

3. **Build simple models**

4. **Test with real users**

5. **Improve with feedback**

6. **Scale and integrate**

Repeat—and **embed the loop** into your product, team, and culture.

12.8 – AI for Entrepreneurs and Retail Startups

If you're building a new business:

- **Start with data strategy**: Collect structured customer and inventory data from day one.

- **Build lightweight AI features**: Use APIs like OpenAI, Google Cloud, or Shopify's AI features.

- **Focus on one niche problem**: Solve personalization, product search, or fulfillment in one category.

- **Be transparent with customers**: Ethics and privacy will become differentiators.

AI isn't a buzzword—it's your strategic weapon.

12.9 – Industry Collaboration & Networking

Communities and Networks:

- Retail Innovation Club

- AI in Retail Slack Groups

- LinkedIn Groups for Retail Tech

- NRF (National Retail Federation) Future of Work events

- Meetup.com: AI in Business chapters

Conferences:

- ShopTalk

- Retail Innovation Conference

- AI Summit

- CES (Consumer Electronics Show)

- NRF Big Show

These venues provide exposure to tools, talent, and partners.

12.10 – Personal Growth in the AI Era

Ask yourself:

- What part of retail am I most passionate about?

- What AI tools are shaping that space?

- How can I become the **bridge** between tech and retail?

- How can I learn continuously and share what I learn?

The AI economy rewards curiosity, collaboration, and **action**.

12.11 – Conclusion: Your Role in the AI Retail Future

AI is not just a technology—it's a movement. A shift in how retail works, how careers grow, and how companies compete. Those who embrace this shift—not fear it—will thrive.

Whether you're guiding a multinational retailer, managing a local shop, or just starting your journey into retail tech, the message is clear:

- Learn AI

- Lead ethically

- Build smart

- Stay human

You are the future of AI in retail.

Conclusion

The retail industry stands on the cusp of a technological transformation unprecedented in its history. Throughout this book, we have explored how **Artificial Intelligence (AI)** is no longer a futuristic add-on, but a core driver of modern retail strategy. From merchandising to customer service, AI has consistently shown its power to make retail more efficient, more personalized, and more responsive to trends. In these chapters we've seen AI algorithms analyze massive datasets to forecast demand with uncanny accuracy, power dynamic pricing models that adjust in real time, and fuel recommendation engines that tailor product suggestions to each customer's unique tastes. The result is a more dynamic, efficient, and customer-centric retail landscape than ever before.

At the heart of this transformation is the **customer experience (CX)**. AI has enabled retailers to truly know and serve their customers across all channels. E-commerce websites and mobile apps now leverage machine learning to create personalized storefronts for every shopper, displaying products and promotions curated to individual preferences. In physical stores, technologies like computer vision and sensor-equipped **smart shelves** keep inventory in check and ensure popular items are always in stock. **Chatbots** and voice assistants handle routine inquiries instantly, giving shoppers 24/7 support and freeing human staff to focus on complex or high-touch service. This symbiosis of AI and human workers means shoppers enjoy faster, more convenient, and more engaging interactions — whether they're online, in a store, or hopping between the two in an **omnichannel** journey.

While celebrating these advances, we have also acknowledged the critical challenges and responsibilities that come with AI integration. **Data privacy** emerged as a central concern: retailers must safeguard the sensitive customer information that fuels their AI systems and comply with regulations like GDPR to maintain public trust. We discussed issues of **bias (in AI)** and the importance of using diverse, representative data to train AI models so that automated decisions — from product recommendations to credit approvals — are fair and inclusive. **Transparency** in AI operations is equally vital. Both customers and employees need to understand, at least in broad terms, how AI-driven conclusions are reached. By embracing ethical AI practices (such as explainable AI tools and audits for bias), retailers can ensure that their use of AI aligns with company values and societal expectations. In essence, the successful future of AI in retail will not be measured by technology alone, but by the trust it earns from consumers.

Another recurring theme has been the role of people alongside AI. Rather than replacing humans, the most effective retail AI solutions **augment** employees' abilities. AI excels at handling repetitive, data-heavy tasks — updating price tags across thousands of products or scanning through hours of surveillance footage — tasks that would be tedious or impossible at scale for people. This efficiency empowers retail employees to shift toward higher-value activities such as building relationships with customers, creating visually appealing merchandising displays, or strategizing the next big campaign. Training and change management are crucial in this transition. We examined how retailers are investing in upskilling their workforce, teaching staff to interpret AI-driven insights (like advanced analytics dashboards) and to collaborate with intelligent automation (for example, using **robotics** in warehouses or working with AI-assisted point-of-sale systems). The takeaway is clear: the future of retail work is one of **human-AI collaboration**, where intuition, creativity, and empathy from people combine with the precision, speed, and scale of AI. Businesses that effectively blend these strengths are poised to lead in the coming years.

Looking ahead, the **future of AI in retail** is filled with opportunities. Emerging technologies promise to blur the lines between the digital and physical shopping realms, creating a truly **"phygital"** experience. Imagine stores where augmented reality mirrors let customers virtually try on outfits or preview how furniture would look in their living room. We are already seeing early versions of this, and as **augmented reality (AR)** and **virtual reality (VR)** mature, such experiences will become commonplace. **Generative AI** models, like those behind conversational agents and content-creation tools, are poised to take retail personalization even further — automatically generating tailored marketing messages, product descriptions, or even designing new products based on consumer trends. In logistics and fulfillment, AI will continue to optimize every step of the supply chain: warehouses run with self-learning robots, **last-mile delivery** routes plotted by AI for maximum speed and sustainability, and predictive systems that adjust stock levels preemptively when they sense market shifts or seasonal changes. Crucially, these innovations won't happen in isolation. They will feed into each other — data from smart IoT devices in stores will inform AI demand forecasts; insights from social media **sentiment analysis** could influence real-time production decisions. Retail is evolving into a high-tech ecosystem, and AI is the connective tissue knitting that ecosystem together.

In conclusion, **AI in retail** is not an end in itself but a means to an end: delivering greater value to customers and businesses alike. The retailers of tomorrow will be those who harness AI's capabilities to create richer, more personalized customer journeys while operating with extreme efficiency and foresight. But in doing so, they must also remain vigilant stewards of their customers' trust, using AI responsibly and ethically. The final lesson of this book is one of balance. Embrace innovation, but remember the human element; leverage data, but protect it fiercely; automate decisions, but guide them with strategy and conscience. The story of AI in retail is still being written, and its chapters ahead are filled with promise. By applying the insights and best practices discussed in these pages, retail leaders can navigate this exciting transformation with confidence. Together, human expertise and artificial intelligence will shape a retail experience that is smarter, more seamless, and more inspired than ever before – an evolution that benefits everyone from the stockroom to the storefront to the satisfied customer at home.

Index

A

B

C

D

Glossary

Algorithm: A set of rules or instructions that a computer follows to solve a problem or make a calculation. In the context of AI, algorithms process data step-by-step to learn patterns or make decisions (for example, a formula that determines which products to recommend to an online shopper).

Artificial Intelligence (AI): The broad field of computer science aimed at creating machines capable of intelligent behavior. AI systems can perform tasks that typically require human intelligence – such as learning from data, recognizing patterns, understanding language, or making decisions. In retail, AI powers everything from smart product recommendations to automated inventory management.

Augmented Reality (AR): A technology that overlays digital content (images, information, etc.) onto the real world through a camera view or AR glasses. In retail, AR allows customers to virtually "try on" clothes, see how furniture would look in their home, or get additional product info by pointing a smartphone at an item in a store.

Automation: The use of technology to perform tasks with little or no human intervention. Automation in retail can range from simple rule-based systems (like an automatic reorder trigger when stock is low) to advanced AI-driven processes (such as robots sorting packages in a warehouse). The goal is often to increase efficiency, reduce errors, and free up humans for more complex work.

Bias (in AI): A tendency of an AI system to produce outcomes that are prejudiced or skewed due to **biased data** or design. For example, if a product recommendation AI is trained mostly on data from one demographic, it might unfairly favor choices for that group. Retailers try to eliminate bias in AI to ensure recommendations, credit decisions, or personalized offers are fair and inclusive for all customers.

Big Data: Extremely large sets of data that are collected and analyzed to reveal patterns or trends. In retail, "big data" might include millions of transaction records, online clicks, social media comments, and more. AI techniques are often applied to big data because the volume is too vast for manual analysis – for instance, using big data to detect shopping trends or optimize store locations.

BOPIS (Buy Online, Pick Up In Store): A shopping model where customers purchase products online and then pick them up at a physical store or designated pickup point. BOPIS is a popular omnichannel retail strategy that combines e-commerce convenience with immediate pickup. AI can assist BOPIS operations by forecasting which store locations need to stock certain online-purchased items and optimizing pickup scheduling.

Brick-and-mortar: A common term referring to traditional physical retail stores (buildings made of brick and mortar), as opposed to online stores. Brick-and-mortar retail involves in-person shopping experiences. AI technologies are helping brick-and-mortar stores remain competitive by enabling features like smart shelves, cashierless checkouts, and in-store personalized promotions to bridge the gap with online shopping.

Chatbot: A conversational program (often powered by AI) that interacts with users via text or voice. Retailers use chatbots on websites or messaging apps to answer customer questions, provide product recommendations, assist with orders, and even handle basic customer service issues. Modern AI chatbots understand natural language and can simulate a friendly, helpful sales associate available 24/7.

Cloud Computing: The delivery of computing services (such as data storage, servers, databases, and software) over the internet ("the cloud"). Instead of running programs on local computers, retailers often use cloud computing to host AI models and data. This allows heavy data processing (like analyzing shopper behavior across all stores) to be done on powerful remote servers, and the results can be accessed from anywhere. Cloud platforms by providers like Amazon, Microsoft, and Google are commonly used to deploy retail AI solutions.

Computer Vision: A field of AI that enables machines to interpret and understand visual information from the world (such as images or video). In retail, computer vision is used for things like recognizing products and their positions on store shelves, enabling **facial recognition** for store security or personalized greetings, powering self-checkout systems that identify items, and analyzing shopper movements through a store to glean insights about store layout effectiveness.

CRM (Customer Relationship Management): A strategy and set of tools for managing a company's interactions with current and potential customers. In practice,

CRM often refers to software databases that track customer data (purchase history, preferences, service tickets, etc.). AI enhances CRM by analyzing this data to find patterns — for example, predicting which customers might respond to a certain promotion, or automatically personalizing marketing emails based on individual shopping behavior.

Cross-selling: A sales strategy of suggesting or selling additional products related to the one a customer is already considering or has in their cart. (For example, recommending a laptop sleeve and mouse when someone buys a laptop.) AI systems in retail excel at cross-selling by analyzing buying patterns ("Customers who bought X also bought Y") and presenting relevant add-on suggestions in real time, both online and at point-of-sale in stores.

Customer Experience (CX): The overall quality of a customer's interactions with a brand across all touchpoints and channels. This includes everything from browsing a website, to shopping in a store, to after-sales service. A great customer experience in retail is often seamless, personalized, and satisfying. AI contributes to improving CX by enabling personalization (tailored recommendations and offers), reducing friction (fast checkout processes, voice search, etc.), and ensuring help is always available (through chatbots or proactive support).

Customer Lifetime Value (CLV): A metric that estimates the total value (usually in revenue or profit) a customer will bring to a business over the entire span of their relationship. In retail, knowing a customer's CLV helps businesses decide how much to invest in marketing and service for that individual. AI can aid in calculating CLV by analyzing purchase histories and predicting future spending, and can also help increase CLV by identifying high-value customers and targeting them with loyalty programs or exclusive offers.

Data Analytics: The process of examining raw data to draw conclusions and inform decision-making. In retail, data analytics might involve studying sales numbers, foot traffic counts, or website clicks to understand what's happening in the business. AI takes data analytics to the next level by automating the discovery of patterns or anomalies that humans might miss – for example, flagging an unusual surge in demand for a product or finding hidden correlations in customer purchase habits.

Data Privacy: The practice of handling sensitive data (like personal and financial information) with care and protecting it from unauthorized access. In retail, data privacy means safeguarding customer data – names, addresses, credit card numbers, purchase history, and more. With AI systems processing so much customer data (for personalization, marketing, etc.), retailers must ensure robust privacy measures: secure data storage, encryption, compliance with privacy laws, and transparency with customers about how their data is used.

Deep Learning: An advanced subset of machine learning that uses multi-layered **neural networks** (somewhat analogous to layers of neurons in the human brain) to learn complex patterns from large amounts of data. Deep learning has driven major improvements in AI capabilities like image recognition and natural language understanding. In retail, deep learning might be behind a visual search feature (interpreting an image of a product), a voice assistant understanding a spoken request, or a demand forecasting model recognizing intricate patterns in sales data.

Digital Transformation: The process of integrating digital technology into all areas of a business, fundamentally changing how the business operates and delivers value to customers. In retail, digital transformation might include moving from paper records to digital systems, adopting e-commerce and mobile shopping, and of course leveraging AI and data analytics at the core of decision-making. The goal is often to become more agile, data-driven, and customer-centric in an increasingly digital world.

Dynamic Pricing: A strategy where product prices are not fixed but instead adjust in real time based on various factors — such as demand, inventory levels, competitor pricing, time of day, or even customer segments. Online retailers frequently use dynamic pricing algorithms (a form of AI) to optimize prices and maximize sales or profits. For example, an AI might lower the price of a slow-selling item to stimulate demand or raise the price of a high-demand item when stock is running low.

Edge Computing: Computing that is done near the source of the data, i.e., on local devices or servers *at the "edge"* of the network, rather than sending data back to a centralized cloud server. In a retail setting, edge computing might involve in-store processing — for instance, a camera in a store aisle using an on-board AI chip to analyze footage and alert staff of low stock **in real time**, without needing to upload video to the cloud. Edge computing can make AI applications faster and more efficient by reducing latency (delay) and easing bandwidth demands, which is especially useful for real-time retail operations like checkout or security monitoring.

Facial Recognition: A technology (often powered by computer vision AI) that can identify or verify a person's identity from a photo or video frame of their face. In retail, facial recognition might be used for security (identifying known shoplifters or unauthorized visitors), or for customer service personalization (recognizing VIP customers to alert staff). It's a controversial tech due to privacy concerns, and retailers using it must consider legal regulations and public perception.

Fraud Detection: The use of processes and tools to identify fraudulent activities, such as stolen credit cards, false returns, or cyber-hacking attempts. AI has become a key tool in fraud detection for retail, especially online. Machine learning models can analyze transaction patterns and spot anomalies that suggest fraud (for example, an unusual purchasing spree on a credit card, or a batch of suspicious e-commerce orders from one address). By catching fraud early, retailers protect their revenue and their customers.

Generative AI: A category of AI systems designed to generate new content that is similar to the data they were trained on. Examples include AI models that can write text, compose music, or create images. A well-known generative AI application is **ChatGPT**, which can produce human-like text responses. In retail, generative AI is beginning to be used for tasks like creating product descriptions, generating personalized marketing content, or even designing new fashion items by analyzing current trends and coming up with novel designs.

Internet of Things (IoT): A network of interconnected physical devices that can collect and exchange data over the internet. These "smart" devices – such as sensors, smart appliances, RFID tags, or cameras – often work in tandem with AI to enable automation and insights. In retail, IoT devices are everywhere: smart shelves that detect when inventory is low, beacons that send offers to your phone as you walk by, climate sensors that adjust store heating/cooling, and so on. The data from IoT devices can feed into AI systems to optimize store operations and the shopping environment.

Inventory Management: The supervision and control of a retailer's stock of products – knowing what is in stock, what is on order, what's selling fast, and what's sitting on shelves. Good inventory management ensures that the right products are available at the right time, without overstocking or stockouts. AI greatly improves inventory management through **inventory optimization**: forecasting demand for each item, automatically reordering stock when levels get low, and even repositioning products to the best locations. For example, an AI system might predict a surge in umbrella sales due to an upcoming storm and prompt stores to stock and display them accordingly.

Last-mile Delivery: The final step of the delivery process where a product reaches the customer's doorstep. It's often the most expensive and time-consuming part of the shipping journey (involving local vans, bike couriers, or drones rather than large trucks). AI plays a growing role in optimizing last-mile delivery by plotting more efficient delivery routes, consolidating orders smartly, predicting delivery times, and even guiding autonomous delivery robots or drones. For retailers, mastering last-mile delivery means faster shipping for customers and lower logistical costs.

Loyalty Program: A marketing program offered by retailers to reward frequent customers. Shoppers typically enroll (often via an app or membership card) and earn points, discounts, or special perks based on their purchases. AI enhances loyalty programs by analyzing the rich customer data these programs provide – helping retailers personalize rewards (e.g., giving a discount on a product a customer often buys), predict which lapsed customers might be re-engaged with an offer, or even create individualized loyalty tiers. The result is a loyalty program that feels tailor-made for each member, increasing customer satisfaction and retention.

Machine Learning (ML): A subset of AI in which algorithms improve automatically through experience. In other words, ML algorithms learn patterns from *training data* and use those patterns to make predictions or decisions on new data. Instead of being explicitly programmed with fixed rules, an ML system (like a model that recommends products) will "train" on historical examples of customer behavior and iteratively adjust itself to get better at its task. **Supervised learning, unsupervised learning**, and **reinforcement learning** are all types of machine learning. In retail, ML drives personalization (learning what products to show you), demand forecasting, pricing optimization, and countless other predictive tasks.

Natural Language Processing (NLP): A branch of AI focused on enabling computers to understand, interpret, and generate human language. NLP allows AI to make sense of text or voice inputs. In retail, NLP is what powers voice search ("Find me black sneakers under $100"), smart assistants like Alexa, and chatbots that can comprehend and respond to customer questions. Effective NLP means a more natural, conversational interaction between customers and AI systems, whether through typing or speaking.

Neural Network: A computational model inspired by the human brain's network of neurons. It's composed of layers of interconnected "nodes" (artificial neurons) that process data by assigning weights and passing signals forward. Neural networks are the foundation of many modern AI applications, especially **deep learning**. For example, an image recognition neural network might take pixel data as input and, through many network layers, determine with high accuracy whether that image contains a shoe or a shirt. In retail, neural networks might be used in a model that takes all of a customer's browsing and purchase data to predict the next product they're likely to buy.

Omnichannel: A retail strategy that provides customers with a seamless shopping experience across all channels, whether they are shopping online via a website, using a mobile app, or visiting a physical store. "Omnichannel" means the boundaries between channels blur – a customer might research a product on their phone, test it in a store, and buy it later on their laptop, with each step feeling like part of one unified journey. AI supports omnichannel retail by connecting data from all these channels: for instance, recognizing that the person who browsed a product online is the same person in the store, and then giving a consistent recommendation or ensuring the cart from the website is accessible in the app. By integrating inventories, customer data, and AI-driven insights, omnichannel approaches ensure that customers receive consistent and personalized treatment no matter how they interact with the brand.

Personalization: Tailoring the shopping experience to the individual customer's preferences and behavior. This can include showing personalized product recommendations, targeted promotions, custom homepages, or even individualized emails and coupons. AI is the engine behind modern personalization in retail — machine learning models crunch customer data (purchase history, browsing activity, demographics) to predict what each shopper is most interested in. The result is that no two customers necessarily see the same retail experience; each gets a curated journey designed to increase relevance and satisfaction, which often leads to higher sales and loyalty.

Phygital: A buzzword derived from blending "physical" and "digital," referring to experiences or strategies that combine aspects of physical retail with digital technology. A phygital approach means using digital tools to enhance in-store experiences (like interactive kiosks, AR try-ons, or mobile apps used while in a store), or bringing tangible, store-like elements into the digital realm (like virtual showrooms or 3D product views online).

The concept recognizes that the best retail strategy often merges offline and online strengths. AI plays a role here by linking the data and intelligence across both realms — for example, an AI might recommend a product online and also inform the local store so that when the customer walks in, an associate or a smart sign can highlight that product.

Planogram: A schematic or plan for where and how products should be placed on retail shelves or displays to maximize sales (a **merchandising** plan). Creating an effective planogram involves deciding which products go next to each other, how many facings they get, and at what shelf height. AI helps retailers optimize planograms by analyzing sales data, shopper eye-level patterns, and even image data of shelves to find the most effective layouts. Additionally, with computer vision, AI can check **planogram compliance** – i.e., verify that stores have arranged products as directed and alert managers if something is out of place or needs restocking.

Point of Sale (POS): The time and place where a retail transaction is completed – in other words, where the customer pays for their purchases. This could be a cash register in a physical store or a virtual checkout cart on an e-commerce site. POS systems typically include hardware (like a card scanner or tablet) and software (sales transaction and inventory software). Modern POS systems are increasingly smart: they might incorporate AI to suggest upsells to a cashier ("The customer buying a camera might want to hear about a memory card deal") or to analyze purchasing patterns in real time. Data from POS transactions is also fed into AI systems for analytics on sales and inventory.

Predictive Analytics: The use of data, statistical algorithms, and machine learning techniques to identify the likelihood of future outcomes based on historical data. It's about forecasting "What's likely to happen?" In retail, predictive analytics can forecast demand (predict how many units of an item will sell next week), predict customer churn (which customers are unlikely to return, so proactive offers can be made), or anticipate trends (which product categories will be popular next season). AI enhances predictive analytics by handling huge data sets with many variables and finding complex patterns that traditional analysis might miss, thus improving the accuracy of these predictions.

Predictive Maintenance: A proactive maintenance strategy where AI analyzes data from equipment (machines, vehicles, refrigerators, etc.) to predict when a breakdown or failure might occur, so that maintenance can be done just in time to prevent it. In a retail context, predictive maintenance can apply to things like HVAC systems in stores, refrigerators in a supermarket, or delivery trucks in a fleet. Sensors (part of IoT) might monitor temperature, vibration, or performance metrics, and an AI model learns what patterns signal an upcoming problem (for example, a slight motor vibration change might precede a refrigerator failure). By fixing or tuning up equipment before it breaks, retailers avoid downtime, save on costly emergency repairs, and ensure a smooth shopping experience.

Recommendation Engine: A system (usually powered by AI algorithms) that suggests products or content to users based on analysis of data. In retail, recommendation engines are the technology behind those "You might also like…" or "Customers who viewed this ultimately bought…" sections on websites and apps. They work by analyzing user behavior (browsing, searching, past purchases) and sometimes comparing it to millions of other users to find patterns. For example, a recommendation engine might learn that people who buy item A and B are likely to enjoy item C, and thus recommend C to someone with A and B in their cart. These engines boost sales and enhance personalization by helping customers discover products that fit their needs and tastes.

Reinforcement Learning: A type of machine learning where an algorithm learns by trial and error, receiving *rewards* or *penalties* for the actions it takes, and using those to gradually improve its strategy. It's often used for decision-making problems. In retail, reinforcement learning could be used for complex tasks like pricing optimization (the AI "tries" different pricing strategies in a simulated environment to see which yields the best profit without losing customers) or personalized offers (learning what sequence of offers keeps a customer most engaged over time). Over many simulations or time periods, the reinforcement learning agent aims to maximize its cumulative reward (for instance, overall profit or customer lifetime value).

RFID (Radio Frequency Identification): A technology that uses small tags and radio waves to identify objects. Each RFID tag contains a tiny chip and antenna and can be attached to products or packages. In retail, RFID tags are used to track inventory automatically – when an RFID reader scans a room or shelf, it can detect all tagged items and know exactly what (and how many) products are there, without needing line-of-sight as barcodes do. This enables quick inventory counts, finding misplaced items, and even automated checkout in some cases. AI systems can integrate RFID data to get real-time inventory updates and trigger actions (like reordering stock or notifying staff to restock a shelf) immediately.

Robotics: The design and use of robots – machines capable of carrying out complex actions automatically. In retail, robotics has multiple applications: **warehouse robots** that move and sort products (for example, robotic arms or autonomous forklifts in distribution centers); **in-store robots** that roam aisles to check inventory or assist customers (some stores have rolling robots that scan shelves for missing products or clean the floors); and even customer-facing robots in some cases (like robotic baristas or security robots). AI is what gives many modern robots their "brains," allowing them to navigate, recognize objects, and make basic decisions. By employing robotics, retailers can speed up operations, reduce labor for repetitive tasks, and sometimes create novel shopping experiences.

RPA (Robotic Process Automation): Software technology (not a physical robot) that automates repetitive, rules-based tasks by imitating how a human would interact with computer systems. RPA in retail is often used for back-office operations – for instance, an RPA bot could automatically transfer online order data from a webstore to an old inventory management system that isn't directly integrated, or it could generate routine reports and email them out. While not "intelligent" in the learning sense, RPA is very effective at saving time and eliminating human error for tedious processes like data entry, invoice processing, updating product info across multiple systems, etc. Increasingly, RPA is being combined with AI (in what's termed "intelligent automation") to handle more complex workflows.

Sentiment Analysis: A technique used to determine the emotional tone behind a series of words, often to understand the attitudes, opinions, or feelings expressed. In retail, sentiment analysis is commonly applied to customer feedback — for example, analyzing product reviews, social media comments, or survey responses. AI-driven sentiment analysis can quickly sift through thousands of tweets about a brand and tell the retailer what percentage are positive, neutral, or negative, and even identify key themes customers are happy or unhappy about. This helps retailers react faster to public opinion, address issues, and gauge how well products or campaigns are being received emotionally by the audience.

Smart Shelves: Store shelving equipped with sensors (and sometimes cameras) that detect information about the products on them. A typical smart shelf can sense the weight or presence of products — so it knows when stock is low or an item has been removed. More advanced versions use computer vision to actually "see" product facings and gaps. These shelves then communicate data to the store's system: alerting staff to restock, triggering automatic reorders via AI, or even enabling features like automatic checkout (as seen in some checkout-free store concepts). Smart shelves are part of IoT in retail and make inventory management in physical stores far more efficient and accurate.

Supervised Learning: A common machine learning approach where an algorithm is trained on **labeled data** (data that already has correct answers provided) so that it can learn to predict the labels on new, unseen data. It's like learning by example with a teacher. In retail, an example of supervised learning would be training an AI model on a dataset of past customer transactions labeled as "churned" or "loyal," so the model can learn to predict which current customers are likely to churn. Each training example includes both the input (customer's behavior metrics) and the desired output (whether they churned), and the model adjusts itself until it can output the right labels reliably. Many AI applications in retail — like demand forecasting, fraud detection, or product classification — are built with supervised learning models.

Supply Chain: In retail, the supply chain refers to the entire network and process of producing and delivering goods, from raw materials all the way to the consumer's hands. It encompasses manufacturers, wholesalers, warehouses, transportation, and retail stores. Managing the supply chain means coordinating all these steps so that the right products are made and delivered at the right time, in the right quantity. **Supply chain optimization** is where AI comes in: using algorithms to make this flow as efficient as possible. AI can analyze factors like lead times, supplier reliability, weather, and consumer demand to optimize ordering (when and how much to reorder), choose the best shipping routes, and minimize costs while avoiding stockouts. A well-optimized, AI-assisted supply chain can respond quickly to changes (like a sudden surge in demand or a disruption at a factory) with minimal manual intervention.

Transparency (in AI): The quality of an AI system being understandable and open in how it works or makes decisions. Transparency helps build trust – both for internal stakeholders and customers – that the AI is doing the right things for the right reasons. In retail, AI transparency might mean clearly explaining to customers how their data is being used to recommend products, or a company auditing its AI pricing algorithm to ensure it isn't unfairly raising prices on certain shopper groups. Techniques for AI transparency include using **explainable AI** (XAI) tools that can, for example, show which factors most influenced an AI decision (like highlighting that price and brand were the key factors in a product recommendation). In summary, transparency is about avoiding a "black box" scenario; instead, retailers strive to keep AI decision-making as open and interpretable as possible.

Unsupervised Learning: A type of machine learning that deals with unlabeled data. Here, the AI is not given explicit correct outputs; instead, it tries to find patterns, groupings, or structures in the data on its own. Unsupervised learning is often used for **clustering** and **segmentation**. In retail, an example would be feeding an unsupervised algorithm tons of customer records and having it segment shoppers into distinct groups purely based on purchasing patterns (without being told what those groups are ahead of time). The AI might discover, say, a group of customers that only shop during holidays, or a group that buys primarily eco-friendly products. These insights can then inform marketing strategies (even though the AI wasn't explicitly told what to look for). Unsupervised learning can reveal hidden affinities in data that humans weren't aware of, providing fresh perspectives on customers and products.

Upselling: A sales technique of encouraging a customer to purchase a more expensive item, an upgrade, or an add-on to the product they're considering, thereby increasing the value of the sale. For example, if a customer is looking at a 32-inch TV, an upsell might suggest a 42-inch model with better features, or when buying a phone, the upsell could be the next model up with more storage. AI assists with upselling in retail by identifying when to prompt an upsell and what to offer: it can analyze a customer's past behavior and the context to determine if they might be willing to consider a premium option, and then highlight that option either online ("Upgrade to the Pro version for $100 more") or to a sales associate who can mention it.

Virtual Reality (VR): A technology that immerses users in a completely computer-generated environment, typically through a VR headset that covers the eyes (and sometimes ears and hands with controllers). In a retail context, VR can create simulated stores or showrooms that customers can explore from home. For example, a home improvement retailer might offer a VR app where you can virtually walk through a kitchen you designed with their products, or a clothing retailer might create a virtual catwalk experience. While still an emerging area for retail, VR experiences, often coupled with AI, aim to provide that sense of "being there" when you physically can't be – potentially making online shopping more experiential.

Visual Search: An AI-driven search method where a user can upload or snap a photo of an item, and the system tries to find similar products or the exact match in a catalog. Instead of typing keywords, the search query is an image. For instance, if you see a chair you like at a café, you could take a picture and use visual search to find that chair (or similar ones) at furniture retailers. This relies on computer vision to analyze the image's features and match them to product images in a database. Visual search is increasingly offered by fashion and home décor retailers, recognizing that customers often know what they want when they see it, even if they can't describe it in words.

Voice Assistant: A digital assistant that interacts via voice commands and responses. Examples include Amazon's Alexa, Google Assistant, and Apple's Siri. These assistants use AI (particularly NLP and voice recognition) to understand spoken questions or commands and respond with useful information or actions. In retail, voice assistants enable **voice commerce** – customers can search for products, check order statuses, or even make purchases using voice commands (e.g., "Alexa, order more laundry detergent"). Retailers are starting to integrate with voice platforms so that their customers can shop or get support hands-free. A voice assistant in a shopping app might also guide a user through a purchase by voice or answer detailed product questions in a conversational manner. Voice technology adds convenience and accessibility to the shopping experience for users who prefer speaking over typing.

www.ingramcontent.com/pod-product-compliance
Lightning Source LLC
LaVergne TN
LVHW022338060326
832902LV00022B/4120